The Biblical Seminar

PROBLEMS AND PROSPECTS
OF
OLD TESTAMENT THEOLOGY

Problems and Prospects of Old Testament Theology

Jesper Høgenhaven

jøt

1988

jsot press

To the Queen's College, Oxford

Copyright © 1987 Sheffield Academic Press

Published by JSOT Press
JSOT Press is an imprint of
Sheffield Academic Press Ltd
The University of Sheffield
343 Fulwood Road
Sheffield S10 3BP
England

Typeset by Sheffield Academic Press
and
printed in Great Britain
by Billing & Sons Ltd
Worcester

British Library Cataloguing in Publication Data

Høgenhaven, Jesper
    Problems and prospects of Old Testament
    theology.— (The Biblical seminar; 6)
    1. Bible. O.T.—Criticism, interpretation,
    etc.
    I. Title   II. Series
    221.6   BS1171.2

    ISBN 1-85075-180-7

CONTENTS

PREFACE

This monograph is not in the proper sense a survey of the field of Old Testament theology. The reader who primarily looks for information about major trends and viewpoints must be directed to one of the instructive recent surveys which are available. In particular, Gerhard F. Hasel's *Old Testament Theology: Basic Issues in the Current Debate* (2nd edn; Grand Rapids, Michigan, 1975), and Henning Graf Reventlow's studies, *Hauptprobleme der alttestamentlichen Theologie im 20. Jahrhundert* (Erträge der Forschung, 173; Darmstadt, 1982 [ET, *Problems of Old Testament Theology in the Twentieth Century*, London, 1985]), and *Hauptprobleme der Biblischen Theologie im 20. Jahrhundert* (Erträge der Forschung, 203; Darmstadt, 1983), deserve to be mentioned.

What we present here are some reflections on basic problems that face the discipline of Old Testament theology. These problems, however, can most conveniently be discerned, and most easily be understood when certain aspects of recent scholarly discussions are examined. The first part of the book, therefore, offers a highly selective analysis of the post-war debate on Old Testament theology.

There are, it seems, basically two ways in which one may speak of a debate on Old Testament theology. In a more limited sense, one may think of a particular theological discipline and of the debate to which this discipline may give occasion. Then the debate is concerned with questions such as the purpose and method of the discipline, relations between Old Testament theology and other disciplines, and the like. In a broader sense the debate is concerned with all important theological questions regarding the Old Testament. These may be questions about the theological concerns of the Old Testament writers, about creation and redemption in the Old Testament, or about the ways in which Old Testament wisdom literature or Old Testament prophets look upon God and man. Or they may be problems such as the Old Testament as canon, its authority and present-day relevance, its place in the preaching of the Church, and so forth. The broader understanding, in effect, makes it impossible to draw any sharp dividing line between Old Testament theology and Old Testament hermeneutics.

Now the problems concerning Old Testament theology in the strict sense, the discipline of Old Testament theology, are hardly comprehensible if they are not viewed against the background of contemporary Old Testament theology in the broader sense. It is not, therefore, advisable to confine oneself entirely to dealing with the problems of Old Testament theology as a particular discipline. However, these questions are the main concern of the present study.

The reader will find that certain debates between German Protestant scholars in the 1950s are discussed here in particular detail. The reason for this is that in my opinion this is where some of the basic problems of Old Testament theology were most thoroughly and fruitfully worked through. I have drawn particular attention to contributions by Friedrich Baumgärtel, whose work has for many years not received the attention it deserves, and especially to the debate between him and Gerhard von Rad.

The second part of the book attempts to present a comprehensive view of the basic problems of biblical theology, naturally presupposing their preceding examination in Part I. After a discussion of principles, I shall conclude by sketching a tentative model for an Old Testament theology, which has as its background the present state of Old Testament studies.

Jesper Høgenhaven
Copenhagen, May 1986

ACKNOWLEDGMENTS

The present work is a revised version of a prize essay written for the University of Copenhagen (1983/84). I wish to thank my examiners, Prof. Eduard Nielsen and Dr John Strange, for their constructive and inspiring criticism, and the editors of Sheffield Academic Press, Prof. David J.A. Clines and Dr Philip R. Davies, for accepting the book for publication.

I am particularly indebted to Prof. Ernest W. Nicholson for his ever encouraging interest in my work, for his most gracious assistance in correcting and improving both the contents and the style of the book, and, above all, for his personal kindness towards me.

I gratefully record my thanks to the Faculty of Theology in Copenhagen for the financial support which made possible my sojourn in Oxford in 1983-84, when the original, Danish version was composed. My special thanks are due to my supervisor during that year, Dr Preben Wernberg-Møller, for his stimulating suggestions and criticisms, and for extending to me his hospitality and friendship. Of great importance for my work was the daily exchange of thoughts and ideas with friends and companions at the Queen's College. Out of a large number of people I wish here to mention Messrs Gianluigi Oliveri and Stefan Rebenich, to both of whom I remain, not only gratefully indebted, but attached through bonds of intimate friendship.

Jesper Høgenhaven
Rome, October 1987

ABBREVIATIONS

ANET	*Ancient Near Eastern Texts Relating to the Old Testament*
ATD	Das Alte Testament Deutsch
AThANT	Abhandlungen zur Theologie des Alten und Neuen Testaments
BEvTh	Beiträge zur evangelischen Theologie
BHTh	Beiträge zur historischen Theologie
BKAT	Biblischer Kommentar Altes Testament
BWANT	Beiträge zur Wissenschaft vom Alten und Neuen Testament
BZAW	Beihefte zur Zeitschrift für die alttestamentliche Wissenschaft
ET	English translation
EvTh	*Evangelische Theologie*
FRLANT	Forschungen zur Religion und Literatur des Alten und Neuen Testaments
IDB	*Interpreter's Dictionary of the Bible*
JSOT	*Journal for the Study of the Old Testament*
JTS	*The Journal of Theological Studies*
KuD	*Kerygma und Dogma*
NS	New series
RHPhR	*Revue d'historie et de philosophies religieuses*
SBT	Studies in Biblical Theology
SJT	*The Scottish Journal of Theology*
StTh	*Studia Theologica*
ThLZ	*Theologische Literaturzeitung*
ThSt	Theologische Studien, Zürich
ThZ	*Theologische Zeitschrift*, Basel
VT	*Vetus Testamentum*
VTS	Supplements to *Vetus Testamentum*
WA	Martin Luther, *Werke*. Kritische Gesamtausgabe (Weimarer Ausgabe)
WMANT	Wissenschaftliche Monographien zum Alten und Neuen Testament
ZAW	*Zeitschrift für die alttestamentliche Wissenschaft*
ZSTh	*Zeitschrift für systematische Theologie*
ZThK	*Zeitschrift für Theologie und Kirche*

PART I
SOME PROBLEMS IN THE POST-WAR DEBATE
ON OLD TESTAMENT THEOLOGY

Chapter 1

HISTORICAL SURVEY

Before we turn to some main problems in recent debate on OT theology, a preliminary survey of the chronological course of the debate will be appropriate. This survey is intended merely as a background for the following thematic discussion, in order that viewpoints and controversies may be located within an approximate historical framework. It pretends to be nothing but a rough sketch, which should, however, allow us to gain an impression of the most important stages in the debate on OT theology since World War II.

Since the endeavours of this period can only be understood when the state of theology and, in particular, OT studies in the years immediately preceding are taken into account, a brief section on the inter-war years has been included.

1. *Old Testament Theology between the Wars*

From about 1920 a renewed concern with the theological task of OT exegesis began to make its impact on biblical studies, a concern which was also a reaction against the predominantly 'historical' interest of biblical scholars in the previous period.

Several factors were active in creating this new orientation. Of extreme importance were the endeavours of 'Dialectical Theology', with Karl Barth as the most prominent spokesman. Theologians of this school demanded a theologically conscious biblical exegesis, which was to take seriously the canonical function of Scripture. The rise of Dialectical Theology was linked to a general attack on 'Liberal Theology' and its alleged evolutionism. In the area of OT studies the prevalence of 'historicism', typical of the nineteenth century, was challenged. It should also be noted that OT scholars were themselves arriving at results which seemed to point in a similar direction. This would seem to be true of certain results of form- and tradition-critical analyses, initiated by scholars of the 'History of Religions school' and now carried on along new lines, notably by Gerhard von Rad and Martin Noth. In the light of their studies, the OT literature came to be viewed as *kerygma* and confession.

In this context, the discipline of OT theology was bound to attract renewed interest. The preceding period had tended to handle the discipline 'historically', with the ultimate perspective of OT theology merging in, or becoming identical with, the history of Israelite religion; this was now felt to be unsatisfactory. In 1925, Carl Steuernagel, in a well-known essay, called for a rehabilitation of a systematic OT theology beside the discipline of Israelite religious history. This, however, did not amount to a contrast in principle between 'historical' and 'systematic' aspects. According to Steuernagel, even OT theology had a historical, descriptive task. The difference was that this description was to assume the form of a systematic survey, whilst history of Israelite religion was to trace the development of Israel's religion chronologically.[1] Thus, for Steuernagel, the terms 'systematic' and 'historical' designate synchronic and diachronic perspectives within the framework of historical description. Otto Eissfeldt, in his famous article of 1926, was far more radical. Here 'historical' and 'systematic' perspectives were assigned to entirely different levels—that of knowledge and that of faith, respectively. History of religion has to do with Israelite religion as a historical phenomenon, whilst OT theology deals with divine revelation in the OT. Consequently, Eissfeldt suggested that the two disciplines be left to exist in absolute mutual independence—history of Israelite religion as objective description and OT theology as confessional testimony to the revelatory content of the OT.[2]

Among the 'OT theologies' written between the wars, the three-volume work of Walther Eichrodt most clearly and directly reflected the new orientation of that period.[3] Eichrodt's intention was to present an overall view of the religious contents of the OT, and to do justice to the essential relations between the Old Testament and the New. This approach led Eichrodt to reject the historicism of the nineteenth century.[4] Instead he offered a systematic cross-section of the OT world of thought, and, at the same time, tried to meet the demands for historical perspective in a number of historical surveys of particular themes.

'Theological reconquest of the Old Testament'—thus the programme of the inter-war years might appropriately be described. In Germany the 'Church conflict' ('Kirchenkampf') during the Nazi period came to reinforce this tendency. The programmatic rejection of the OT advocated by radical 'Deutsche Christen' ('German Christians') almost automatically led theologians and churchmen opposed to the Hitler régime to emphasize their confidence in the OT as an indispensable part of Scripture. In general, emphasis on scriptural authority found a favourable climate in the 'orthodox' or 'conservative' mood which characterized the German Protestant churches during the Church conflict and the first post-war years.

'Historical or systematic'—thus the methodological conflict in inter-war OT theology might conveniently be described. As we have seen, the extent and implications of this conflict were not altogether clear. 'Historical' and 'systematic' might indeed signal the fundamental divergence between a theological-normative and a 'neutral'-descriptive perspective, but the same terms were also used merely to designate different functions of historical description.

2. *The Period 1950-1960*

In many respects, Otto Procksch's voluminous OT theology, posthumously published in 1950, was at home in the theological situation before World War II. The introduction attempted to locate OT theology within a theological conception of history with Jesus Christ as its centre, and to settle the relations between theology and history of religion. According to Procksch, the theological perspective was to be given superior rank.[5] Then in two main sections Procksch described the 'historical world' ('Geschichtswelt') and the 'world of thought' ('Gedankenwelt') of the OT, thus in fact combining historical and systematic approaches.

Procksch's work, though widely praised for its scholarly qualities, exercised no great influence on the debate of the following years. This may have been partly due to Procksch's highly conservative historical viewpoints. Very influential, however, was an initiative taken by Gerhard von Rad—who had been responsible for editing Procksch's theology—and a number of other German OT scholars engaged in an ambitious project. Their aim was to publish a new commentary series, in which recently won exegetical and theological insights were to find an adequate expression.

The circle of prominent OT exegetes involved in the project called *Biblischer Kommentar* ('Biblical Commentary') presented their programme in the 1952 issue of the periodical *Evangelische Theologie*, and expressed the hope that the programme might provoke a general debate on fundamental problems of OT exegesis and theology. The programme was contained in a number of essays in which the participants in the commentary project treated questions of exegetical principles and methods. Martin Noth deals with the inevitable gulf between the historical-critical aspect, which sees the OT as a phenomenon of the historical past, and the canonical status of the OT, which implies a demand for its relevance for present-day preaching. Noth attempts, on an exegetical basis, to establish some principles for a legitimate actualization of the OT. He points to the actualization of historical events which takes place in the cultic feasts of ancient Israel, accompanied by narrative 'preaching', and concludes that a legitimate actualization of the OT must consist in a recital of God's saving acts.[6] Gerhard von Rad attempts to rediscover typology as a relevant model for OT interpretation. Criticizing alleged 'spiritualist' tendencies in much modern OT exegesis, he emphasizes that the OT is a 'book of history' ('Geschichtsbuch'), which bears witness to a history determined by God. Von Rad pleads for a typological exegesis which focuses on the concrete events of revelation as they are narrated by the OT, and views these as prefigurations of the Christ-event.[7] In his contribution Walther Zimmerli is concerned with the question of continuity between the Old and the New Testament. He argues that the history presented by the OT is a great movement from promise to fulfilment, in which no one but Yahweh himself is the centre of all promises, and the Christ-event of the New Testament the decisive fulfilment.[8] Hans-Joachim Kraus attempts a critical dialogue wth Jewish interpretations of the OT,[9] and Hans Walter Wolff considers the practical methodology of OT exegesis with Hos. 2.1-3 as example.[10]

When the programme of these scholars is viewed as a whole, it is evident that its background is the new theological orientation of the inter-war period. Their concern is the task of OT exegesis as a theological discipline, or the relevance of the OT for present-day Christian theology and preaching. In this context, the relationship between the Old and the New Testament was necessarily of crucial importance, and the idea of 'typological exegesis' was an attempt at solving this problem. Furthermore, it is clear that the scholars in this commentary project belonged to the German tradition-historical school, and presupposed the viewpoints on OT literature advanced by Noth and von Rad. The OT was essentially preaching, *kerygma*, in the form of historical narrative.

The initiative of the *Biblischer Kommentar* circle met with a marked critical reaction from Friedrich Baumgärtel, Professor in Erlangen, who had long since been dealing with theological problems of OT exegesis.[11] In a recent article Baumgärtel had sketched his understanding of OT theology as a discipline. He assigned two tasks to it, the religion-historical task of describing the contents and character of OT religion, and the strictly theological task of establishing the relevance of the OT for the present-day Christian.[12] In his book *Verheissung* (1952) Baumgärtel elaborated his views at greater length. The book was written before the essays of the *Biblischer Kommentar* circle appeared, but in an appendix Baumgärtel responded to their challenge in a polemical treatment of Zimmerli's and von Rad's essays.[13] The following years saw a lively, at times even heated, debate between Baumgärtel on one side and von Rad and H.W. Wolff on the other.[14] Baumgärtel's basic objection to the *Biblischer Kommentar* circle is that they have neglected to take seriously enough the religion-historical relativity of the OT—and consequently fail to see the real theological problem. Whereas the *Biblischer Kommentar* circle is concerned with the direct relevance of the OT texts for Christian theology and preaching, it is fundamental to Baumgärtel's hermeneutics that Christian theology always has to see the OT in a 'broken' perspective with the gospel of the New Testament as criterion.

An entirely different response was given to the *Biblischer Kommentar* circle by the Dutch systematic theologian Arnold A. van Ruler. In his book *Die christliche Kirche und das Alte Testament* (1955) he criticized the idea of 'typological exegesis', which, he considered, was bound to obscure the proper message of the OT. His intention is the very opposite of Baumgärtel's. Van Ruler wants to emphasize the direct and unbroken relevance of the OT for the preaching of the Church. The OT, according to van Ruler, is to assist the Church in its 'theocratic' mission of reforming society and culture.[15] However, van Ruler's book did not decisively influence the debate, for although references to it are frequent—often, van Ruler is mentioned as a warning example!—its position was too extreme, and the book was too much a piece of dogmatics to gain any broader importance.

As might have been expected, the rehabilitation of typological exegesis attempted by von Rad and Wolff was widely discussed and often heavily criticized. Baumgärtel rejected the idea briskly, viewing it as a dangerous legitimization of arbitrary and unmethodical interpretation.[16] And there were criticisms from Alfred Jepsen and Walther Eichrodt as well.[17] In fact the notion of 'typological exegesis' was soon more or less tacitly dropped, probably because it turned out not to be a particularly useful vehicle for the idea intended by its advocates, as Eichrodt had pointed out.[18]

We have tried to trace some of the main lines in German OT theology of the 1950s. In roughly the same period the English-speaking world saw a marked and in many ways parallel interest in the theological and pastoral relevance of biblical exegesis. The dominant trend in American biblical studies in the 1950s has been termed the 'Biblical Theology Movement'. Its main characteristic was its emphasis on the theological responsibility of scriptural interpretation. Furthermore, Anglo-American biblical studies shared a number of basic viewpoints. The unity of the Bible was stressed, and there was a widespread belief in the existence of a unique biblical 'mentality'. In this last respect great importance was ascribed to the alleged contrast between 'Hebrew' and 'Greek' thought, and in general to the contrast between the contents of Scripture—Old and New Testaments—and the surrounding ancient Near Eastern and Hellenistic cultures.[19]

The debate of the 1950s was reflected in several OT theologies which appeared during the decade. Here we may mention G. Ernest Wright's *God Who Acts* (1952) though it does not carry the title 'OT theology'.[20] Wright's book is an unmistakable product of the 'Biblical Theology' school. Israelite religion with its dynamic-transcendental view of God, founded on his revelation in historical acts, stands in sharp contrast to the static-immanent nature religions of the ancient Near East. The 'theology' of the OT writers is described as the 'recital' of God's saving acts in history, and the present-day discipline of 'biblical theology' should, according to Wright, adopt an essentially similar structure. With his emphasis on the uniqueness of OT religion and his obvious dependence on continental theology and exegesis of the 1920s and 1930s,[21] Wright appears as a typical representative of his school.[22]

An important work of this period was Edmond Jacob's OT theology.[23] Jacob understands OT theology as a historical and descriptive discipline, but his book is 'systematically' arranged. 'Theology' is taken in a rather literal sense to mean interpretation of the OT doctrine of God and his relations with man and the world. In accordance with this 'theocentric' principle, the arrangement of the book comes to resemble the traditional order of dogmatic *loci*. Another notable work was the OT theology by Th.C. Vriezen, originally published in Dutch, which appeared in 1956 in a revised German version.[24] This work, too, follows a 'systematic' plan, and includes an extensive introduction dealing with the fundamental theological problems concerning the OT as a witness to divine revelation.

The programme of the *Biblischer Kommentar* group was most impressively worked out by Gerhard von Rad in his monumental Old Testament theology, of which the first volume, *Die Theologie der geschichtlichen Überlieferungen Israels*, appeared in 1957, and the second volume, *Die Theologie der prophetischen Überlieferungen Israels*, was published in 1961. Without doubt this was the single most influential work in OT theology of the entire period.[25]

It goes without saying that we shall have to return repeatedly to von Rad's work. Consequently, I shall make only some summary remarks here. Von Rad's *Theologie* is based on tradition-historical principles. The object of OT theology, according to von Rad, is Israel's testimonies to Yahweh; and these testimonies consist in references to Yahweh's acts in history, references which were continually passed on, combined, revised, and made relevant for new situations, in the process of tradition. Von Rad attempts to trace this process, and thus he is concerned with the way Israel viewed its own history (in its confession of Yahweh), rather than with the sort of reconstruction of Israel's history that critical scholarship is able to present. In fact, however, von Rad also tries to do justice to such critical reconstruction in a survey of 'the history of Yahwism', which forms the first section of his Old Testament theology.

Methodologically, von Rad's work was an innovation. Compared to the OT theology of Eichrodt, it must be described as a departure from the 'systematic' arrangement. Eichrodt had made the 'covenant' his organizing centre. Von Rad, however, explicitly rejected the possibility of interpreting the OT by means of any conceptional 'centre'. Rather, the process of tradition within the OT was to determine the plan of OT theology.

3. *The Period 1960-1970*

In a twofold sense Gerhard von Rad's *Theologie* had made 'history' a central theme. First, according to von Rad, it was a decisive characteristic of the OT texts that they were concerned with history. Secondly, his OT theology itself followed a historical plan, determined by the OT process of tradition. Thus, von Rad's work gave occasion to a number of complex questions. What was the theological relevance of history? In what sense was it possible to speak of a 'salvation history'? What was the relationship between salvation history, history of facts, and history of tradition?

'Revelation—*kerygma*—history'. Those key words may serve to indicate the essence of the debate on OT theology throughout the 1960s. Obviously this debate is intimately linked to contemporary New Testament studies and systematic theology, and the links would seem to be stronger and of a more direct nature than they had been in the 1950s. In the theological situation of the 1960s '*kerygma* and history' were viewed as the crucial issues. The scene was dominated by Bultmann's programme of 'demythologizing', but there were, of course, contrasting tendencies as well. Among Bultmann's own disciples, a new quest for the 'historical Jesus' soon materialized. The idea of 'salvation history' was advocated by more conservative New Testament scholars like Oscar Cullmann and Ethelbert Stauffer, and the 'universal history' programme was associated with the Wolfhart Pannenberg school. However, the fact that the basic problems were the same gave a certain sense of unity to the theological endeavours of the 1960s. At least this appears to be the case when the period is seen in retrospect. Biblical scholars and systematic theologians were conscious of being engaged in the same fundamental problems, although this by no means resulted in generally agreed solutions.

The field of OT theology was dominated by the debate on von Rad's work, but the problems it raised were in fact the questions also on the general agenda of contemporary theology.

Though von Rad's OT theology was universally recognized as a work of outstanding importance, there was no shortage of criticism. F. Baumgärtel wrote a long review, which was—not surprisingly—very critical, accusing von Rad of lacking logical methods and conceptual clarity. In particular, von Rad was said to have no consistent idea of revelation, and according to Baumgärtel, this was the reason why he failed to address the real theological problem of the OT.[26] In fact, with Baumgärtel's review the discussion between him and von Rad came to an end.[27]

Other critics also found von Rad in want of clarity. Franz Hesse argued that von Rad was in effect engaged in history of religion study rather than theology. Von Rad's exposition of Israel's 'testimonies' is to be seen as a history of religion. Theology, according to Hesse, must be concerned with 'real', factual history, and not (or not primarily) with Israel's testimonies to history. Theologically, 'salvation history' must be concerned with factual history, i.e. events which have actually taken place, and these can be approached only through critical research.[28] Similar objections were voiced by Henning Graf Reventlow, who argued that von Rad was avoiding theological responsibility by confining himself to investigating ancient Israel's testimonies. Von Rad had failed to realize that the centre of the OT is the God of revelation, whilst Israel's testimonies are merely the human response to revelation.[29]

Theologians of the 'existentialist' school were in general united against von Rad's basic ideas. In principle, this school was suspicious of any theological project which included the notion of 'salvation history'. One partisan of this phalanx, Martin Honecker, produced a penetrating analysis of von Rad's understanding of history, and pointed out its fundamental ambiguity and some of the problems which then arise.[30] Another representative of 'existential theology' was Hans Conzelmann, who found it necessary, against von Rad, to emphasize the fundamental difference between OT and NT revelation.[31]

Others, however, tried to develop von Rad's viewpoints further, and to carry out his programme more stringently than he had himself done. This is true, above all, of the group of younger German theologians who found their leader in Wolfhart Pannenberg. As we have seen, F. Baumgärtel criticized von Rad for lacking a consistent idea of revelation. In 1961, that is, at the same time as the publication of von Rad's second volume, the Pannenberg circle presented their programme in a collection of essays entitled *Offenbarung als Geschichte*.[32] The book was an attempt at a systematic investigation of the concept of revelation. Revelation, according to the Pannenberg school, was to be understood as God's revelation of himself in history. This necessarily led to the idea of a 'universal history', for only when seen as a whole, from its final point, could history be a full revelation of God. The focus on history as the *locus* of revelation is common to the Pannenberg circle and von Rad, and the circle explicitly claimed that they had received decisive inspiration from von Rad, and were attempting to carry on his intentions.

The 'Revelation as history' programme soon made its impact on OT theology. Rolf Rendtorff, in a study of OT ideas of revelation, attempted to demonstrate that the OT found Yahweh's revelation in historical acts. Furthermore, Rendtorff argued that there was a development in Israel's view, in the sense that Yahweh's definitive revelation came to be understood more and more as a future act.[33] These views caused a discussion between Rendtorff and Walther Zimmerli, who pointed to the 'word' rather than the historical event as the primary vehicle of revelation in the OT.[34] Klaus Koch's endeavours to interpret the origins of Israelite Yahwism within the context of universal religious history—as opposed to claims of a 'unique' origin for Israelite faith—was also in line with Pannenberg's theology. Koch rejected the notion of a historical person as the 'founder' of Israelite religion.[35] Against this view F. Baumgärtel felt compelled to make a stand in defence of more traditional positions.[36]

While the debate was dominated by sharply contrasting positions, which mainly derived their profiles from contemporary divisions in systematic theology, there were authors who strove to find a *via media*, and to combine elements from different conceptions. Friedrich Mildenberger tried to integrate different perspectives, and to view the unity of Old and New Testaments as a 'history of preaching' ('Verkündigungsgeschichte').[37] Likewise, F. Hesse criticized both von Rad's and Pannenberg's versions of tradition-historical interpretation, and, continuing Baumgärtel's intentions, proposed to see the relevance of the OT under the heading 'promise'. Here both 'historical' and 'existential' models of interpretation were to be granted a legitimate role.[38] In later works, however, Hesse modified his views, and finally came to reject any theological use of 'salvation history', thus aligning himself more closely with the positions of 'existential theology'.[39]

In Anglo-American theology the 1960s saw an increasing collapse of the Biblical Theology Movement which had dominated the preceding decade. This was partly due to the erosion of some of its basic historical and exegetical assumptions, such as the uniqueness of Israelite 'mentality'.[40] At the same time, new and more 'liberal' tendencies were making their impact on the English-speaking theological world, partly surpassing the 'neo-orthodox' orientation in systematic theology, which had formed a natural background for the Biblical Theology Movement.[41]

4. *The Period after 1970*

When von Rad died in 1971, his exegetical and theological studies had long been exercising a decisive influence both on his followers and on his critics. An impressive testimony to the importance of his work was the *Festschrift* in his honour which appeared that same year, and which contained contributions by biblical scholars and systematic theologians of many different opinions.[42]

However, OT scholarship in the early 1970s was marked by a general move away from established positions. Martin Noth's theory of an ancient Israelite amphictyony, for a long time an object of criticism, was now abandoned by an increasing number of scholars. Theories about the origin and early history of Israel were thrown into the melting pot again, but no new reconstruction appeared capable of gaining general acceptance. Lothar Perlitt's attack on the idea of the 'covenant' as the basis of Israelite religion throughout its history made a remarkable impact.[43] In the area of Pentateuch research, there were loud demands for a revision of current views. One thinks, for example, of Rolf Rendtorff's work, questioning the existence of the 'Yahwist' as a literary source with a particular theology in the sense Pentateuchal criticism had hitherto assumed,[44] or of Hans Heinrich Schmid's challenge to the early dating of the Yahwist proposed by von Rad.[45] In fact, these scholars were now adopting viewpoints which had earlier on been characteristic of Scandinavian scholarship.[46] All in all, old and venerable bastions were shaken, and this obviously affected some of the basic assumptions which had supported OT theology in previous years.

It was a characteristic feature of this new situation that the wisdom literature was increasingly focused on by OT scholars. This literature, which had formerly often been relegated to the periphery of OT studies, was now increasingly recognized as being of central importance within the history of Israelite religion. Gerhard von Rad's last book was typical of the time in this respect.[47]

The new orientation in OT studies was accompanied by changes in the theological climate as a whole. It is hard to avoid noticing that the sense of essential solidarity between biblical and systematic studies which had prevailed in the 1960s—despite all the hermeneutical problems—began to dissolve after 1970. Systematic theology seemed increasingly inclined to go its own way, engaged in questions unrelated to biblical exegesis. 'Political Theology'—an important factor in the 1970s—adopted a clearly pragmatic and eclectic attitude to the Bible. Scripture may be important as, for example, a source of inspiration and useful imagery, but biblical foundations are by no means a life or death necessity for theology.

All this meant that OT theology in the 1970s came to find itself, once more, in a rather isolated position. To be sure, its links with systematic theology were not broken. An example of continued mutual influence is the increasing interest in OT wisdom, which partly reflects a new theological situation in which human experience and analyses of nature and society are emphasized as valid sources of religious knowledge, whilst the exclusive 'revelation' emphasis of dialectical and existential theology is widely dropped.[48]

The interest in clarifying the fundamental problems of OT theology, and in establishing its tasks and conditions, is due in part to the new situation of the discipline.

In his book *Biblical Theology in Crisis* Brevard S. Childs described the dominant trends in English and, in particular, American biblical theology in the post-war years, and proposed a programme for a new biblical theology, which was to recognize the canon of the Christian Church as the 'proper context' for biblical exegesis.[49] In Germany, a similar task was undertaken by Hans-Joachim Kraus.[50] The greater part of his monograph (which appeared in 1970, the same year as Childs' book) is a historical survey which attempts to trace the development of 'biblical theology' since the Reformation. In a concluding section, Kraus tries to define the aims for future work in that field.

There were, in other words, various attempts at making 'biblical theology' the programme of the 1970s.[51] This, obviously, signalled a wish to depart from the 'isolated' disciplines of either OT theology or NT theology, and to reach a comprehensive theological approach to the Bible as a whole. This wish, of course, was by no means new, for as we have seen, the unity of the Bible was an important theme in the 1950s, and 'biblical theology' had also earlier been launched as a slogan for a comprehensive approach.[52] However, that this way of phrasing the problem—'Is a proper biblical theology possible?'—was felt to be particularly urgent in the 1970s, was probably because of the altered conditions in which OT theology found itself. There was deep concern about biblical and systematic studies losing contact with each other—and it is exactly the problem of how these disciplines are to be related which is contained in the quest for a 'biblical theology'.

Thus, in a sense there was a certain formal agreement regarding the programme. On the other hand, attempts at executing that programme differed widely in their motives and methods. Hartmut Gese tried to develop the tradition-historical line of von Rad's theology further, and to obtain a comprehensive 'biblical' view by inserting Old and New Testaments into one tradition-historical perspective.[53] Others, critical of tradition-historical approaches, renewed the quest for a unifying 'centre' of the OT. Rudolf Smend argued that the 'covenant formula', the central importance of which had been recognized already by Wellhausen, was to be regarded as the 'centre' of the OT.[54] The problem was then taken up by Zimmerli, who—with his usual analytical and exegetical skill—made the point that Yahweh was himself the 'centre' of the OT unifying its variety of testimonies without ever placing his revelation at man's disposal.[55]

The 1970s saw a renewed theological interest in the concept of 'canon' and in the associated problems.[56] In accordance with the viewpoints of his earlier book Childs proposed to make 'canon' the key concept in a theological approach to the OT. The status of the OT as canonical Scripture of the Church must be the point of orientation and the criterion for its interpretation.[57] This programme, however, received sharp criticism, notably from James Barr.[58]

The unity of Scripture was an important interest behind the various endeavours in biblical theology. In current attempts at including in biblical interpretation insights from contemporary literary methods, we may detect a parallel motive. The studies of the Canadian literary critic Northrop Frye represent an attempt to view the Bible as a literary whole, which as such is of immense importance for understanding Western civilization.[59]

The publication of von Rad's *Theologie* was followed by almost ten years' pause in the stream of OT theologies. For obvious reasons it cannot be determined whether this pause was in fact due to the impact of von Rad's work, but undoubtedly his 985 pages may well have caused ambitious successors to lose their nerve. Then in the 1970s a flood of OT theologies appeared, and we shall conclude our chronological survey by mentioning some of the most important.[60]

Georg Fohrer's OT theology, published in 1972, is again a clearly 'systematic' work.[61] Fohrer attempts to analyse the 'existential attitudes' ('Daseinshaltungen') of the OT writers. The essence of the OT, according to Fohrer, is the 'prophetic attitude' of faithful submission to God's will, an attitude which surmounts all 'magic, cultic, legalistic, and nationalistic' tendencies. We also find materials systematically arranged in Zimmerli's work (1972), in which he sums up results and viewpoints from his extensive and very fruitful exegetical endeavours.[62] Zimmerli's OT theology, which has since appeared in revised editions, is in line with his earlier works. Beginning with the name of Yahweh, Zimmerli follows a 'theocentric' plan, with due consideration of historical and tradition-critical problems.

Ronald E. Clements' OT theology (1978) is 'systematic' in the same sense.[63] The first part deals with the OT doctrine of God and his people, and is followed by tradition-critical studies of 'law' and 'promise' in the OT. Chapters on the theological relevance and importance of the OT form the framework of the book. In his OT theology from the same year, Claus Westermann has arranged his materials according to the triple structure of the Masoretic canon ('law', 'prophets', and 'writings').[64] Westermann deals with God's saving and blessing activity, his judgment, and man's response in word and deed. His OT theology appears as a balanced work, in which both the 'salvation history' aspect is maintained, and consideration given to recent theological emphasis on themes like creation and the immanent structures of the world.

5. Concluding Remarks

In the post-war debate on the OT the 1950s appear as the really creative period, for this was when most of the basic questions concerning the historical relativity of the OT, as opposed to its present-day canonical relevance, were formulated, and the various alternative solutions were proposed. In fact, the problems and attempted solutions of the 1950s have delivered much, if not most of the material for the discussion of the following decades. At the same time, however, the presuppositions of the debate, and the general climate in which it takes place, have been decisively altered, both theologically and exegetically. In the area of OT research Noth's and von Rad's conceptions of ancient Israelite origins and history, and of the literary process behind the OT, have been shown to be precarious. As for the broader theological situation, dialectical theology and existential theology have to a great extent been replaced by different schools of thought. Naturally, this development has changed the conditions of OT theology; the basic questions, on the other hand, by and large remain the same.

Chapter 2

THEMES AND PROBLEMS

In this chapter we shall examine in more detail problems of major importance in the post-war debate on OT theology. The problem of method which is of particular interest to us will be dealt with in the first section. The problem of identifying a 'centre' of the OT, some formal or material principle or point of orientation by means of which the structure of OT theology might be defined, is in fact one side of the methodological problem. Since, however, 'the centre of the OT' has been the theme of a particular discussion, this question will, for practical reasons, be dealt with separately. Some space will have to be devoted to the central issue of the relationship between the Old Testament and the New, and in close connection with this main theme we shall also treat 'canon' and 'biblical theology'.

Since this is not, strictly speaking, a historical survey, I shall make no attempt at an exhaustive (and for the reader inevitably exhausting) presentation of viewpoints held by a great number of scholars. Instead, I have selected certain characteristic authors as representative of main trends.

1. *The Method of Old Testament Theology*

As mentioned above, OT theology inherited some unsolved fundamental problems from the inter-war period. Was OT theology a historical or a systematic discipline? This might, as we have seen, be merely a question of how to arrange the materials. But it might also be a problem with much wider implications, a question of how to differentiate Old Testament theology from the history of Israelite religion, and of assessing the relationship between these disciplines.

These questions, it may be added, are as old as the discipline of OT theology itself. From a historical viewpoint, OT theology came into being as a branch of 'biblical theology' and it is a well-known fact that the origins of this discipline are inseparably linked to the problem of 'historical' and 'systematic' theology. In fact, the famous programme of Johann Philipp Gabler defined 'biblical theology' as a *historical* discipline as opposed to systematic theology.[1]

It is not possible here to analyse all or even the most important OT theologies written after World War II, in order to assess how the methodological problems have been solved. Instead, I have chosen two works as representative of the main tendencies. The OT theologies by Otto Procksch and Gerhard von Rad offer a characteristic representation of the 'systematic' and the 'historical' orientation, respectively, and will serve to elucidate the motives behind both orientations, as well as the advantages and problems arising from them. A consideration of a more practical nature may be added. Both Procksch and von Rad have dealt explicitly with problems of methodology, and, consequently, their methodological principles may be more easily and directly assessed than those of many others.

A. *Otto Procksch. The 'systematic' solution*

In his introduction Procksch takes up the problem of 'historical' and 'systematic' approaches. The question, according to Procksch, is how to define the relationship between 'theology of history' ('Geschichtstheologie') and 'history of religion' ('Religionsgeschichte').[2] In a footnote he alludes to the methodological debate of the inter-war years.[3] How does Procksch understand these concepts and their relationship?

In order to arrive at an answer, it will be necessary to follow the progress of Procksch's rather complicated argument. His introduction has the following sections: 1. Theology of history. 2. Theology of the OT. 3. Theology of history and history of religion. 4. History of the theme (i.e. the theme of OT theology). The first section begins with this statement:

> All theology is Christology. Jesus Christ is the only subject in the world of our experience, in which God's revelation is complete. God is in Christ, and Christ in God, this relationship between God and man is absolutely unique in history, it is not repeated in any other subject.[4]

Christ is the revelation of God, which has taken place in history, and

which, consequently, binds us to history, making history the theme
of theology. In Christ theology recognizes the centre of all history.[5]
Procksch goes on to explain what is implied by this theological
perspective on history. Theology views Christ as the omnipresent
centre, both in relation to the 'macrocosm' of history, i.e. the
Church, and to its 'microcosm', the individual Christian. Theology is
also able to recognize an 'analogy of faith' ('Analogie des Glaubens')
which unites all Christians, notwithstanding the historical and
cultural distances that separate them. Finally, history in the
theological perspective includes the eschatological expectation of a
second coming of Christ.[6]

Apparently, for Procksch 'theology of history' is really a definition
of theology. All theology must necessarily be historical. This follows
from Procksch's Christological point of departure. The historical
revelation in Christ has in a sense made history the proper
dimension of theology. 'Theology of history', then, is not some
special branch of theology, but rather a description of theology as it
should be. Procksch's remarks about history in the theological
perspective illustrate what this 'theology of history' ought to look
like. Theology is an interpretation of history, which assumes that
Jesus Christ is the centre that gives history a meaning, and makes it
an organic whole.[7]

Procksch's second section attempts to locate the discipline OT
theology within this framework. The following considerations serve
to establish the theological relevance of the OT. Without the OT as
historical background the ministry of Jesus Christ is incomprehensible.
Jesus, on the other hand, viewed his own person as the fulfilment of
the OT promise, and this means that the OT is also incomprehensible
without Jesus Christ. If he is left out of consideration, the OT
becomes 'an enormous fragment, a torso without a head'.[8] The God
of the OT is the same as the Father of Christ, and Israel has the same
basic structure as the new people of God, though the latter is
different in being universal.[9]

The third section deals with the relation between 'theology of
history' and 'history of religion'. Theology, according to Procksch,
has two necessary premises, the 'recognition of revelation in Christ'
('die Anerkennung der Offenbarung in Christo') and the 'participation
of faith in historical judgments' ('die Anteilnahme des Glaubens am
geschichtlichen Urteil').[10] Revelation is God's immediate commu-
nication of himself to man, which, however, always includes an

element of mystery, and is recognizable only to faith.[11] And faith must also 'participate' in historical judgments. By this Procksch means that a Christian is necessarily personally involved in the persons and events of Holy Scripture.[12]

These two basic presuppositions, recognition of the revelation, and personal involvement of faith, are not shared by history of religion, which views the Old and the New Testaments in the same way as other religious documents.[13] Therefore the religion-historical approach to the Bible must be deemed inadequate by theology. Nevertheless, theology is able to make religion-historical perspectives useful for its own purpose. Through his revelation God has somehow bound himself to history. The faith of the OT people of God found its expressions in historical forms which are open to religion-historical analysis. In the Old and the New Testaments the 'treasure' of faith is contained in 'earthern vessels'. Thus, according to Procksch, full justice is done to history of religion *within* the framework of theology.[14]

The overall perspective, in other words, remains theological. History of religion may have an instrumental function within this context. One is tempted to say that for Procksch history of religion is a sort of *ancilla theologiae*.

As a consequence of this, Procksch goes on to mantain that OT theology must have a 'vertical' and a 'horizontal' task to perform. It has to examine the historical forms of God's revelation, and their development, and then to analyse the world of thought in the OT in a 'cross-section'.[15] The first of these tasks is 'religion-historical', the second is 'theological', although theology in fact determines the perspective of both.

Procksch, it would seem, regards theology and history of religion as disciplines competing with one another. They treat the same subject matter, but work with different premises. Procksch's solution is to choose theology as the only proper and adequate approach to the Bible. Recognition of the revelation, and a personal believing involvement are prerequisites for understanding Scripture adequately. Within this theological framework Procksch wants to combine 'historical' and 'systematic' arrangement of the material.

Procksch has been criticized for not carrying out his own 'Christological' programme. Such criticism, however, is hardly appropriate. It is true, as critics have pointed out,[16] that the rest of Procksch's OT theology contains no explicit references to the

'Christological' statements of his introduction. But when we follow Procksch's own line of thought, this criticism of his work may be based upon a misunderstanding. His 'Christological' considerations are meant to establish the theological relevance of history, and the historical nature of theology. Because of the historical revelation in Christ, history can be regarded as an organic whole with Christ as its centre, and theology necessarily has to do with *this* history. To Procksch, therefore, the sentence 'all theology is Christology' means simply that all theology must be 'theology of history', interpretation of history which presupposes revelation and faith. Therefore, when Procksch investigates the OT historically, this is an *implicitly* 'Christological' endeavour, according to his own premises. Thus, when the *function* of Procksch's 'Christological' introduction is properly understood, it becomes clear that Procksch does in fact remain faithful to his own programme.

This is not to say that the methodological solution offered by Procksch is not open to criticism. Actually, it would seem to imply a highly problematic understanding of theology. To say that theology presupposes recognition of the revelation is, of course, a very general statement, which may well be appropriate and acceptable, but needs to be more precisely explained. Particularly dubious, though, is Procksch's claim that a personal involvement of faith is a prerequisite for doing theological exegesis. Is it really acceptable to make subjective faith a precondition of theology?

Moreover, one may ask what the consequences will be when this principle is applied to scriptural exegesis. It might, for example, be taken to imply that theological interpretation of the Bible is a sort of 'exclusive' enterprise, and that biblical scholars are allowed to make exegetical statements which cannot—in principle—be verified by way of appealing to the recognizable contents of the texts, but only by way of appealing to personal, subjective faith. Now this, of course, touches on hermeneutical questions concerning the subjective element present in any interpretation, questions we do not intend to deal with here. The important point is the danger of theology becoming dependent on 'esoteric' interpretations of Scripture, instead of being based on facts which are—in principle—'there' in the biblical texts for anyone to see. It need hardly be said that Procksch cannot be accused of having had such ideas in mind, but some of his viewpoints may, if they are taken to extremes, be able to produce consequences of the type mentioned.

Then again, Procksch's way of determining the relationship between OT theology and history of religion implies certain historical and exegetical assumptions which are at least questionable. Procksch assumes that in the OT we have an invariable and somehow definable content as well as some historical forms which are subject to alterations. He quotes the words of Martin Luther: '*Externa variant, interna manent*'.[17] This sentence, it would seem, is the basis of Procksch's distinction between 'religion-historical' and strictly 'theological' functions of OT theology. Now, only by examining the OT texts themselves is it possible to assess whether there is in fact such an invariable theological core in the OT, which can, for analytical purposes, be separated from the changing forms of religious history. As the debate on the 'centre' of the OT has shown, there are grave difficulties involved in all attempts of this sort. In other words, if the 'changing forms' of Israelite religion are to be the domain of religion-historical research, there may eventually be little left to OT theology.

B. *Gerhard von Rad. The 'historical' solution*
In his reflections on the method of OT theology,[18] von Rad also attempts to establish a proper distinction between history of religion and theology. Making use of the available sources it would, von Rad states, be perfectly possible to draw a tolerably complete and objective picture of Israelite religion, of the peculiarities of Israel's conception of God and his relation to man, and so forth. This, however, is in itself a task for the general study of religion. Theology has an entirely different task.

> The subject-matter which concerns the theologian is, of course, not the spiritual and religious world of Israel and the conditions of her soul in general, nor is it her world of faith, all of which can only be reconstructed by means of conclusions drawn from the documents: instead, it is simply Israel's own explicit assertions about Jahweh. The theologian must above all deal directly with the evidence, that is, with what Israel herself testified concerning Jahweh, and there is no doubt that in many cases he must go back to school again and learn to interrogate each document, much more closely than has been done hitherto, as to its specific kerygmatic intention.[19]

Thus, for von Rad the task of OT theology consists in dealing directly with the testimonies or the 'confessions' of Israel, i.e. the

documents of the OT. It is *not* the task of the OT theologian to use
these documents as a starting-point for reconstructing the religious
world of ancient Israel. With an unmistakable allusion to the
concepts of Procksch mentioned above, von Rad says that the subject
of OT theology is the 'world made up of testimonies' and not a
'systematically ordered "world of the faith" of Israel'.[20]

This way of distinguishing between history of religion and
theology may at first glance seem somewhat peculiar. It is perfectly
comprehensible, however, if it is assumed that von Rad works with
the Protestant doctrine of scriptural authority as his implicit
premiss. Then theology is bound to the contents of the biblical texts
themselves, which exercise a normative function, and, consequently,
it is inappropriate for the theologian to depart from these texts to
something different, e.g. to a reconstruction of the development of
Israelite religion. Later, we shall have to return to this point, which
we regard as a very important factor in von Rad's theology.

According to von Rad, it is a feature common to the OT
documents, or, to use his own expression, 'Israel's testimonies', that
they represent Yahweh's relationship to Israel and the world 'in one
aspect only, namely as a continuing divine activity in history'. This
reference to history unites the narrative and the prophetic writings,
and it is present, explicitly or by implication, everywhere in the OT
except for a few particular books (Job, Ecclesiastes). In von Rad's
view, the very lack of historical reference in these books is a symptom
showing that their relationship to the essence of OT faith is
problematic.[21]

The task of OT theology is to explain the 'testimonies' of Israel.
When attempting to solve this task, the OT theologian immediately
has to face the difficulty that the OT is not a systematic survey.
Rather, it tells of Yahweh's revelation in a number of separate
historical acts without exhibiting a 'centre' which would render a
theological systematization of these narratives possible.[22] This,
according to von Rad, is due to some very specific features of Israelite
thinking. 'From first to last Israel manifestly takes as her starting-
point the absolute priority in theology of event over "*logos*".'[23] This
is not to say that Israel was incapable of proper theological thinking.
Only, the 'theological' achievement of Israel mainly consists in the
reworking, rearrangement, and continual reinterpretation of historical
traditions.[24] This process of tradition is not arbitrary, but has its
unity in the idea of 'Israel' itself. 'Here at last we come upon one

unifying principle towards which Israel's theological thinking strove, and with reference to which it ordered its material and thought; this was "Israel", the people of God, which always acts as a unit, and with which God always deals as a unit'.[25] This 'Israel', however is an ideal, or, to use von Rad's own terminology, an 'object of faith'. The historical traditions of the OT were shaped as a result of Israel's constant reflection upon herself. 'Each generation was faced with the ever-identical yet ever-new task of understanding itself as Israel. In a certain sense, every generation had first to become Israel.'[26] Therefore, the traditions handed down had to be made relevant for each new generation through reshaping and reinterpretation. The most conspicuous results of this activity are the great historical complexes of the OT, the Hexateuch, the Deuteronomistic history, and the work of the Chronicler.[27]

This process of tradition is what the OT theologian should attempt to trace and to explain. The task of OT theology is to unfold the 'testimonies' of Israel, and, consequently, its interest has to focus on the historical events as they were understood and interpreted by Israel. 'Thus, re-telling remains the most legitimate form of theological discourse on the Old Testament'.[28]

In practical terms, this means that von Rad's OT theology is structured according to tradition-historical principles. The first volume is devoted to Israel's historical traditions. The foundations are laid through investigations of the various bodies of traditional material in the Pentateuch, and of the motives behind them. Under the heading 'Israel's Anointed' the traditions of Israel's history after the settlement in Canaan are dealt with, and in this connection the theologies of the Deuteronomists and the Chronicler are analysed. In a separate section entitled 'Israel before Jahweh (Israel's Answer)' von Rad addresses cult lyric and wisdom literature. The second volume deals with Israel's prophetic traditions. After an extensive general introduction the prophets of the OT are dealt with in chronological order. The concluding section has as its theme the relationship between the Old Testament and the New. Evidently in this version the discipline of OT theology is characterized by a high degree of affinity with the discipline of OT introduction.[29]

If von Rad's work is viewed with the methodological debate of the inter-war years as background, it is obvious that he represents a return to the 'historical' disposition of OT theology, and expressly rejects the idea of a 'systematic' arrangement. In von Rad's eyes all attempts at drawing a 'cross-section' of the OT world of thought, as in the works of Eichrodt and Procksch, necessarily lead to neglecting the intentions of the OT texts themselves.

Nevertheless, it is also very obvious that it is by no means von Rad's aim to have OT theology replaced by religion-historical description. Certain critics have claimed, though, that despite his own intentions this is in effect what he does. In particular, von Rad's idea of OT theology as 're-telling' or as unfolding the 'testimonies' of Israel has provoked such criticism. Von Rad's 're-telling', it has been alleged, is a re-telling, not of the acts of God, but of Israel's re-telling of these acts.[30] Thus von Rad concerns himself with the products of Israel's faith, but fails to address the real theological problem, which has to do with the alleged divine reality behind that faith.[31] In other words, von Rad's whole endeavour lacks direct theological significance; it amounts merely to a study of the OT literature. Or, as one critic phrased it, von Rad's work is in fact an OT introduction rather than an OT theology.[32]

In particular, Franz Hesse has questioned von Rad's way of distinguishing between religion-historical and theological approaches to the OT.[33] According to Hesse, von Rad's distinction is in fact purely artificial. Von Rad claims that the study of Israel's religious development is a task for the religion-historical researcher, whilst the unfolding of the OT testimonies to Yahweh's acts in history is a theological enterprise. Hesse objects that the OT testimonies are not separate from, but a part of Israel's religious history. Thus, von Rad's entire work with all his penetrating investigations of Israel's understanding of history, and of the confessions to Yahweh's historical acts found in the OT, is in reality nothing but *religion-historical* research.[34] Hesse is also aware that the motive behind von Rad's distinction is his conviction that the OT has a direct and immediate authority for Christian theology.[35] I suggested above that von Rad's implicit presupposition is the classical Protestant doctrine of scriptural authority. The canonical status of the OT gives its contents theological relevance, as opposed to all religion-historical hypotheses and reconstructions. This position, however, is challenged by Hesse, who follows F. Baumgärtel's view that the OT can only have an indirect normative function within Christian theology, since it is a witness out of a religion different from Christianity.[36]

Probably the most penetrating criticism of von Rad's theology has been given by Baumgärtel.[37] The lack of conceptual clarity in von

Rad's work, Baumgärtel complains, actually makes it impossible to realize what 'OT theology' means in von Rad's interpretation.[38] It does not become clear whether 'OT theology' means the 'theology' contained in the books of the OT, or the theology which is concerned with the OT. This is due to von Rad's fundamental ambiguity as to the theological authority of the OT. Von Rad does not inform his readers whether or not he regards the 'theological' testimony of the OT as automatically and immediately valid from the point of view of Christian theology, or whether or not the sort of 'theological thinking' that produced the OT picture of history is normative for our theological thinking today.[39] In particular, Baumgärtel attacks von Rad's idea of 're-telling' as the most legitimate way of speaking theologically of the OT.[40] This highly imprecise concept, Baumgärtel complains, oversimplifies and obscures the whole complex of theological problems concerning the OT. Indeed, Baumgärtel continues, it would seem that von Rad confuses the functions of theology and of preaching. The *preaching* of the Church might well be called 're-telling'. *Theology*, however, is given the task of reflecting upon and clarifying the basis of this preaching.[41]

There can in fact be little doubt that Baumgärtel's criticisms contain some very just observations. In von Rad's OT theology there is an undeniable tendency to move from religion-historical to theological statements without clarifying the principles for such transitions. This methodological confusion is due, above all, to the combination of von Rad's 'historical' approach with his view of the OT texts as directly and immediately theologically normative; a view, however, which is not made subject to reflection or elucidation. The outstanding *forte* of von Rad's OT theology lies elsewhere, in its impressive richness on precise exegetical observations, and its everpresent closeness to the texts and their contents.

2. *The 'Centre' of the Old Testament*

While a 'historically' arranged OT theology follows some kind of chronological scheme, it is essential to the 'systematic' solution (in the methodological sense) that certain organizing principles are decided upon. This is true irrespective of whether OT theology is regarded as religion-historical description or as theological confession. In recent debate considerable interest has been devoted to attempts at establishing one principle or organizing 'centre' by means of which the contents of the OT might be arranged in a justifiable and convincing manner.

According to Walther Eichrodt, the 'covenant' was the central concept and the most convenient principle for a systematic description of OT religion. For Eichrodt, it was of great importance that this concept was taken from the OT itself, and not imposed from outside. The covenant, he believed, was fundamental to Israelite religion throughout its history, embodying and expressing the basic and unique structure of Israelite faith.[42]

The central concept of OT theology is defined in an essentially similar, though broader, way by Th.C. Vriezen. 'Communion between God and man' is the fundamental principle of Israelite religion. 'The basis of Israel's conception of God is the reality of an immediate spiritual communion between God, the Holy One, and man and the world'.[43] This 'fundamental point of faith', which unites the Old Testament and the New, is the best point of departure for a systematic OT theology.[44] Vriezen's definition of the 'centre' is thus more open and inclusive than Eichrodt's, and Vriezen avoids binding himself to the covenant idea as the ever valid conceptual expression of what he sees as the basic theme of the OT.[45]

As mentioned above, von Rad's OT theology—over against the period immediately preceding—represented a return to the 'historical' arrangement. In fact, von Rad explicitly rejected the possibility of determining a 'centre' of the OT by means of which the contents of the OT books might be theologically systematized.[46]. In all such attempts von Rad senses a desire to schematize, a desire contrary to the intentions of the texts themselves, the actual manifoldness of which should be respected. The OT contains not 'a theology', but a number of 'theologies' which differ widely in their structures and their ways of arguing.[47]

Von Rad does not deny that Yahweh might be called the 'centre' of the OT.[48] The question is, however, what this type of general statement really says. 'What sort of Yahweh, then, is that? Is it not a Yahweh who, from time to time, hides himself ever deeper from his people in his acts of self-revelation?'[49] If the real unity within the manifold and dynamic testimonies of the OT documents is to be fully appreciated, rigid concepts are of little use. What is needed is an exegetical awareness of the traits 'typical' of Yahwism.[50]

According to von Rad, the most typical feature of the OT, that which unites its different 'theologies', is the process of tradition that lies behind it. This process has the form of a continual reinterpretation of historical traditions determined by the conviction that Yahweh leads history towards its ultimate goal, the fulfilment of his promises.[51] Since it is obvious that this interpretation of the OT view of history is above all based on the historical writings of the Deuteronomists—von Rad explicitly says that Deuteronomistic theology has given the clearest expression to the OT idea of salvation history[52]—critics have claimed that the Deuteronomistic theology of history is actually the 'secret centre' of von Rad's OT interpretation.[53] There can, in fact, be little doubt that von Rad's idea of what is 'typical' of the OT—the ongoing actualization of historical traditions— functions as a criterion for evaluating the OT materials. Consequently, certain parts of wisdom literature and cult lyrics, which appear to have no part in the 'typical' features of the OT, are only allowed to play an inferior role in the tradition-historical whole of von Rad's theology.

Against this background it is interesting to note Siegfried Herrmann's suggestion that Deuteronomy be declared the 'centre' of biblical theology. In Deuteronomy, Herrmann argues, we have a summary of the most central themes in the OT, which point backwards to the essence of Israelite traditions, and forwards to post-exilic developments. Thus, Deuteronomy provides the key to our understanding of Israel's historical traditions, and of the structure of the Pentateuch. It also represents the point of departure for post-Josianic Israelite history and the emergence of Judaism. Deuteronomistic theology has decisively formed and regulated our approach to the OT.[54] It is characteristic that Herrmann with his definition of the 'centre' of the OT merely intends to bring out explicitly what he believes is already contained in von Rad's theology.[55]

Rudolf Smend, in spite of his appreciation of von Rad's exegetical work, is among the OT theologians essentially critical of von Rad's positions. In his monograph *Die Mitte des Alten Testaments* he intended to make possible an escape from von Rad's negative results, and to make a fresh attempt at identifying the 'centre' of the OT.[56] Smend himself pleaded for finding the 'centre' in the name of Yahweh, and, more particularly, in the so-called 'covenant formula', i.e. the sentence 'Yahweh the God of Israel, Israel the people of Yahweh'. The OT is not concerned with God as such, but with God in his relation to man, the relation signalled by the word 'covenant'. This relation is the reason why the OT speaks about God. Yahweh is the first object of the OT testimony, and Israel is the second, the point, of course, being that both belong inseparably together.[57]

Smend's proposal revives a tradition going back to Wellhausen and his generation.[58] There are, as we shall soon see, also contacts between Smend's idea of a centre and Friedrich Baumgärtel's conception of the 'basic promise' in the OT.[59]

A most prominent member of the opposition to von Rad is Georg Fohrer, whose OT theology is in many respects a marked and deliberate contrast to that of von Rad. Fohrer sees the unity of the OT in the dual perspective of the rule of God and of the communion between God and man. Together these two ideas—'divine rule' ('Gottesherrschaft') and 'divine communion' (Gottesgemeinschaft')— form the unifying element in the plurality of theological viewpoints and tendencies found in the OT. Fohrer compares these two principles to the *foci* of an ellipse.[60]

Gerhard F. Hasel criticizes the idea that the contents of the OT may be systematized by means of one central concept or formula. Whatever 'centre' is chosen, there will inevitably be parts of the OT literature which do not fit into the scheme. The only adequate definition of the 'centre' of the OT is that God is himself the one who unifies the manifold voices of the OT. 'That which binds together the manifoldness of the OT testimonies from the beginning to the end is nothing less than the God who has revealed himself in these diverse and varied ways'.[61] That God is himself declared 'the dynamic unifying center of the OT' implies that this centre cannot be used as an organizing principle for a systematic OT theology. The various books and literary genres in the OT must be allowed to speak for themselves, and testify to God's revelation in their own ways.[62] 'It is thus apparent that to speak of God as the center of the OT means to recognize the intensely dynamic nature of this center. It is and can never be static. It is present everywhere either directly or indirectly and is the central inner aspect which binds together the manifold single parts into a unified whole without silencing considerable portions of the OT'.[63]

A similar line is followed by Walther Zimmerli in his reflections on the theme 'centre of the OT'. Despite all the differences, all the books of the OT are directly or indirectly related to Yahweh's name.[64] Here, then, is the centre of the OT, which, however, is not to be understood superficially in analogy with the centre of a circle, but rather as the point that gives a picture the perspective of depth.[65]

Now it is a characteristic feature of the OT that Yahweh breaks down all attempts to take him captive in a static doctrine or conception. Within wisdom literature this becomes apparent in Ecclesiastes and Job. In two independent ways these books mark the collapse of a tendency inherent in wisdom of enclosing reality in fixed standard ideas about God and the world.[66] Likewise, in the revelation narrative in Exodus 3 Zimmerli discovers a strong emphasis on Yahweh's sovereign power. It is through Yahweh's gracious interventions in Israel's history that the people learn who he is; his name is not placed at men's disposal.[67] And in their preaching the prophets maintain Yahweh's liberty against all human attempts at establishing a safe relationship with him—at the same time they proclaim his faithfulness and his mercy.[68] Thus, even for Zimmerli the real 'centre' of the OT is Yahweh himself.[69] In their manifold ways the various 'theologies' of the OT point to this one Lord, who is contained in no human formula and no human image.[70]

When we look at the debate on the 'centre of the OT' from a certain distance, it seems rather difficult to ascertain what it was really about. At least a brief examination of some of the solutions offered shows that they belong to entirely different formal categories. Among the suggested 'centres' are (1) a theological or religion-historical concept or name ('covenant', 'communion between God and man', 'Yahweh'), (2) a theological or religion-historical formula ('Yahweh the God of Israel, Israel the people of Yahweh'), (3) one of the OT books ('Deuteronomy'). Against this background, it seems clear that certain difficulties are contained in the question itself, or the way it is posed.

The problem of identifying a 'centre' of the OT appears at first glance to be derived from the confrontation between a certain task, namely that of writing a systematic description of the contents of the OT, and a certain object, namely the materials of OT literature. The OT, of course, is not a 'book' or a literary unit in the normal sense, but rather an anthology of writings very different in form and contents. In fact von Rad's well-known description of the Pentateuch as a 'baroque formation'[71] may safely be extended to cover the whole of the OT. Against this background the question arises of continuity within that literary complex which we have become used to call 'the Old Testament'.

In other words, the first motive to look for a 'centre' of the OT is the need to organize a systematic presentation of the main contents of the OT documents. There can be little doubt, however, that another motive is involved as well. That motive is the desire to establish the theological relevance of the OT by assessing its 'centre'. In this sense the 'centre' sought after is something like the permanent 'core' of the OT, that which is able to serve theology and preaching in the Christian Church today.[72]

So when attempts are made to identify the 'centre' of the OT, it is important to keep in mind that formally this may mean quite different things. It does in fact seem highly probable that some of the obscurity that marks the debate on this problem is due to a confusion of these different aspects.

The various suggestions, of course, may be roughly divided into two groups according to their predominantly 'historical' or 'theological' interests. Hasel's and Zimmerli's proposals most clearly fall under the 'theological' category. As a consequence, Hasel has to admit— and readily does so—that his 'centre' cannot be used for organizing a systematic OT theology. But is it possible, then, to argue this 'centre' *against* suggestions which are aimed at serving exactly this organizing function?

We must now proceed, however, to examine the problems of principle involved. From a purely *historical* viewpoint it appears somewhat peculiar to demand the identification of a definite 'centre' in order to trace and present the main lines or contents of a body of historical documents. After all, few would demand of an Egyptologist that he should identify the 'centre' of, say, the religious literature of the New Kingdom, or of a literary scholar that he should point to the 'centre' of German literature of the 'Sturm und Drang' period. Nevertheless, both would probably consider themselves perfectly capable of assessing main lines and common features of New Kingdom religious texts and 'Sturm und Drang' literature respectively, and both might well write systematic treatises on their subjects without being bothered by the absence of expressly identified 'centres' of the type which OT theologians have been striving to establish.[73] It is, actually, rather unlikely that the question of a 'centre' of the OT would have been posed in this manner, had it not been for the problem of *theological* relevance. However, methodologically the two problems should be kept apart. The historical question of differences and common traits within the OT literature is something different from the theological question of how the OT can be relevant for present-day theology and preaching.

On the historical level the attempt at establishing a sort of common denominator for all the documents in the OT 'anthology' can hardly be regarded as a very meaningful enterprise in itself. This is not to deny that the various parts of the OT share common traits, as far as their 'message' and their cultural and religious outlooks are concerned. But in order to describe and explain such traits the identification of one particular 'centre' is not required. In fact, the main lines of the OT may probably be much more conveniently presented if the reference to a 'centre'—which is then usually understood as excluding all other possible 'centres'—is avoided. When compared from outside, some of the 'centres' suggested seem actually to point in the same direction. Von Rad's emphasis on the Deuteronomistic theology of history, Smend's plea for the 'covenant formula', and Herrmann's advocacy for Deuteronomy as centre of the OT, all refer, when considered historically, to theological and literary activities in the period shortly before and during the Babylonian exile, thus indicating that this was perhaps the most significantly formative period in the entire historical process from which our OT eventually emerged. This insight, however, is by no means clarified by attempts to argue that one of these suggested 'centres' can be more convincingly demonstrated as being the 'real' or 'proper' centre of the OT. Instead, an examination of the process behind the formation of the OT, and the factors—cultural, theological, historical—involved in it, would seem to be a much more appropriate key to understanding the actual historical unity within larger parts of OT literature.

Theologically, the idea of a 'centre' of the OT may indeed have a certain justification, to which, however, we shall return in Part II.

3. *The Relationship between the Old Testament and the New Testament*

Two main alternatives can be found in recent theological attempts at explaining the relationship between the Old Testament and the New. One type of explanation emphasizes continuity and unity, whilst a second type is mainly concerned with the aspect of discontinuity and contrast. In the period since World War II the former alternative has been most markedly and consistently represented by von Rad and his followers, and will be dealt with here as 'the tradition-historical approach'. The latter alternative, which may for the sake of convenience be termed 'the dialectical approach', since it is usually characterized by its combination of contrast and unity, has found its most prominent advocates in Rudolf Bultmann and, above all, in Friedrich Baumgärtel, who has worked out an elaborate hermeneutical programme on the basis of the 'dialectical' viewpoint.

In this part of the debate on the OT, 'salvation history' is a theme of major importance. Dealing with this theme in a separate section will provide an opportunity to examine the main features of the diverging positions again in a slightly different perspective, and thus, indirectly, to test the results of our previous analyses.

A. *The tradition-historical approach*

Evidently, von Rad's theological approach to the problem 'Old Testament and New Testament' is related to his form- and tradition-historical research. In his well-known monograph on the form-critical problem of the Hexateuch, he attempted to demonstrate that the Hexateuch is the final result of a process of tradition which had as its starting-point the ancient Israelite 'creed'. This 'creed' is a recital of Yahweh's saving acts in the history of the Israelite people from the age of the Patriarchs to the settlement in Canaan. Von Rad believed that the 'creed' was found in its best preserved shape in Deut. 26.5b-9, and that its original home was the cult. Then, in the course of time the 'creed' was reworked and gradually expanded into a large complex of traditions. A decisive step was the insertion of the Sinai traditions, which originally belonged to a different tradition-historical context, and of the primeval history. This, according to von Rad, was the work of the Yahwist, who is viewed as a writer of outstanding theological distinction from the Davidic-Solomonic era.[74]

From the process of tradition which, according to von Rad, lies behind the Hexateuch, some basic features of Israelite faith can be seen. First, Israel's faith rests on Yahweh's acts in history.[75] Secondly, it is characteristic of Israelite faith that the 'saving acts' of Yahweh are never seen as the exhaustive fulfilment of his promises. Israel always remains on its way to new fulfilments, which even in their turn point forwards to fulfilments yet to come.[76] Thus, on the one hand, Israel's 'theological' thinking is concerned with things historical, with traditional materials, yet on the other, it is characterized by the constant reinterpretation of the old in the light of Yahweh's new acts. For example, when the patriarchal narratives are placed in a context which includes the Joshua tradition, they are given a much wider significance than they originally possessed.[77] Very probably, von Rad's emphasis on actualizing reinterpretation of tradition as essential to Israelite faith has to do with his previous research on Deuteronomy, which very clearly exhibits this pattern.[78]

In von Rad's theology the OT prophets are also viewed against a tradition-historical background. The prophets preached on the basis of tradition, yet when it came to the implications of tradition the prophets differed sharply from their contemporaries. According to the prophets, tradition does not guarantee the salvation of Israel. On the contrary, tradition becomes the ground for Yahweh's judgment on Israel. The ancient 'saving acts' of Yahweh have lost their immediate relevance. For the prophets, salvation depends entirely on new acts of Yahweh.[79] However, the prophets can only describe these expected new acts in analogy with the old acts of Yahweh; they expect a new David, a new Exodus, a new Covenant.[80] But their use of tradition is characterized by a striking freedom. They select certain traditions, and make use of them in their preaching, other traditions are passed over in silence, whilst yet others are criticized and rejected. In this connection, von Rad speaks of a 'charismatic-eclectic' procedure.[81]

This 'charismatic-eclectic' reinterpretation—which, according to von Rad, is a basic feature of the process behind our OT—is repeated on a large scale in the NT or, rather, in the way the NT makes use of the OT. In the light of the new saving act of God, his revelation in Christ, the OT gained a new actuality for the early Christians. In this sense, the Christian reinterpretation of the OT is in accordance with the reinterpretations which are going on within the OT tradition itself.[82]

The crucial question concerning the relationship between Old and New Testaments is whether this reinterpretation of the OT undertaken by the NT writers is legitimate and meaningful. In von Rad's eyes, the very fact that this reinterpretation is structurally similar to basic mechanisms of the process behind the OT gives the procedure a certain legitimacy.[83] This does not mean, however, that the problem of Old and New Testaments is solved. Formally and structurally, the NT repeats and continues what is already going on within the OT. But the further question remains whether the NT interpretation of the OT is justified as far as its actual contents are concerned. Von Rad attempts to answer this question through an analysis of the OT understanding of world and man. The OT understands the world and man in 'historical', non-mythological categories, against the background of Israel's experience of God. Therefore, the OT was able to provide the only 'language'—in a comprehensive sense—in which the Christian faith could express itself.[84] And since the language and thought of Israel is determined by the revelation of Yahweh, we are led to recognize in the OT a real preparatory revelation.[85]

According to von Rad, there is also another and more direct relationship between events and persons of Old and New Testaments. In the light of the NT fulfilment, things related in the OT gain the quality of prefigurations.[86] Von Rad speaks of a 'typological' relationship, implying that there is, in fact, an immediate correspondence between OT texts and the gospel of Christ.[87] The sum of all these reflections is, of course, that the Old Testament and the New belong inseparably together. Neither Testament can be properly understood without the other.[88]

We have already mentioned the close connection between von Rad's approach to the problem of Old and New Testaments, and a particular conception of the literary history of the OT and the development of Israelite religion. This conception, however, has been challenged by a great number of Old Testament scholars in recent years. Thus, it has been convincingly shown that the 'historical creed' in Deut. 26.5b-9, which von Rad regarded as the original core around which the narrative materials of the Hexateuch were gradually accumulated, is essentially a piece of Deuteronomistic literature, not so much a 'creed' as a programmatic monition not to forget the great deeds of Yahweh.[89] Then again, serious doubt has been cast upon von Rad's view that the J document can be dated as early as the Davidic-Solomonic period.[90] The question has even been raised whether we can speak of a J source as traditionally conceived of in source analysis.[91] This means that the foundations of von Rad's conception are shaken. It has become very difficult indeed to retain the relatively unified picture of Israelite religion suggested by von Rad. For example, it is hardly possible to claim that the religion of Israel was from its earliest origins bound to Yahweh's saving acts in history, and concerned with reinterpretation and actualization of historical traditions.

In other words, it looks as if 'Old Testament theology' as presented by von Rad is to a great extent really controlled by the theology of the late monarchical and early exilic literature in the OT. To realize this does not by any means automatically diminish the theological value of his work. It is evident that the religious and theological ideas of this relatively late period have left their stamp on considerable parts of the OT, and, consequently, the theology of the Deuteronomistic and Priestly authors may with some justice and to a certain degree be called the theology of the OT. Nevertheless, the historical fact should be noted that the religion of certain Israelite and Judean circles in the seventh and sixth centuries has in this sense gained a normative status within the OT process of tradition. This the OT theologian should certainly acknowledge, refraining, however, from dating back into early pre-exilic times the normative function of Deuteronomistic and Priestly ideas, for example by insisting on reading the eighth-century prophets in the light of the Deuteronomistic theology of history.

This is not the proper place for developing further the criticisms of von Rad which have been raised on the basis of historical and exegetical research. Instead, some strictly theological objections to his work deserve to be mentioned. Theological criticism of von Rad's OT theology has mainly come from the 'existentialist' school, and their most important allegation has been that von Rad exaggerates the degree of continuity between the Old Testament and the New. The unique 'Christ-event' of the NT, it has been argued, is illegitimately included by von Rad in the OT salvation history, and placed on the same level as the 'saving acts' of God in the OT. This, according to von Rad's 'existentialist' critics, represents an impermissible formalization of the gospel to merely one of God's 'saving acts'. Within von Rad's 'linear' conception the NT gospel is not duly respected as a unique, unexpected, and decisive event.[92]

Gerhard von Rad's answer to this criticism mainly consisted in a plea for having his work understood as an attempt at faithful exegesis of the OT texts. His main concern had always been to let the OT speak for itself. It is careful exegetical study, he argued, which leads to recognizing the 'kerygmatic' intentions of the OT texts, and to discovering the idea of a 'linear' salvation history in the OT literature.[93] It cannot be denied altogether that von Rad chose to avoid addressing the theological problem in the proper sense. His attitude is inconsistent, in so far as he intends, on the one hand, to be theologically relevant, and yet on the other, shows himself inclined to escape theological responsibility by claiming to be 'merely' a historical exegete.

In fact, this takes us back to the methodological problems of von Rad's OT theology, and to the question of the theological relevance of historical analyses. Hans Conzelmann, one of the most prominent of von Rad's 'existentialist' opponents, speaks of the 'latent presupposition' in von Rad's work 'that Yahweh, the God represented by Israel in historically conditioned forms of expression, is really— God, and that this presupposition elevates historical description to theology'.[94] Manifestly, if it is von Rad's presupposition that the God confessed by Israel is *God*, then the continuity between the Old Testament and the New is given *a priori*. This continuity, however, cannot be demonstrated by means of religion-historical analysis.

Others have criticized von Rad's combination of tradition-historical approach and typology. The notion of typological correspondence between persons and events in the Old Testament and the New and of 'structural analogy' between God's acts in Old and New Testaments, implies that there is a direct and immediate connection between the Testaments. The consequence of such a view, it has been argued, is that the intermediate history of tradition loses its importance. In other words, tradition-historical and typological approaches do in fact compete with one another.[95]

Against this background, it is scarcely surprising that others have attempted to carry on von Rad's efforts more rigorously. In continuation of von Rad's work, Hartmut Gese is determined to view Old and New Testaments as belonging to one continuous process of tradition and revelation.[96] According to Gese, the OT came into being through a gradual 'canonization' of traditional materials, and Gese emphasizes that this process was still going on in NT times. Thus the NT process of tradition is a direct continuation of the OT process of tradition; in other words, we have to do with one 'biblical' process. To Gese, however, it is of great importance that the growth of the OT tradition was terminated by the NT event. In Gese's own words, 'We arrive at the following thesis. The OT came into being through the NT; the NT forms the conclusion of a process of tradition, which is essentialy unified and continuous'.[97]

The NT concludes and terminates the growth of OT or, rather, of 'biblical' tradition. This is a fact, Gese argues, attested to even by the Jews, who, mainly under the influence of Christianity, brought the growth of the OT to an irreversible end through the final canonization of the OT after 70 AD. However, it is vital to Gese that the OT process of tradition remains a living and growing reality right up to the end imposed on it through the NT. Consequently, the exclusion of the Apocrypha from the Jewish Canon is an impermissible step since it interrupts the continuity between OT and NT traditions. A Christian theologian, Gese states, ought never to accept the Masoretic Canon; indeed, it was a fatal mistake that the Reformers overlooked this perspective and legitimized the 'Pharisaic' reduction of the OT canon.[98]

So Old and New Testaments are included in one 'biblical' stream of tradition. Gese also refers to this stream as the 'continuum of revelation' ('Offenbarungskontinuum').[99] This would seem to imply that the process of tradition somehow embodies the very idea of revelation. The OT process of tradition, Gese claims, is in itself a 'testimony'.[100] In this connection, von Rad is criticized for not being sufficiently consistent in applying his own viewpoints. According to Gese, von Rad is far too much concerned with establishing a *doctrine* of the historical dimension which characterizes the OT testimonies. Instead, the historical development of the OT traditions themselves should be the methodological principle of OT theology.[101]

Contained in the OT process of tradition, as seen by Gese, is a gradual extension of what he calls the 'consciousness' behind the texts. 'The history of tradition is in a certain sense also the history of the consciousness that experiences revelation, and which is endued with an enormous expansion of its realm of reality'.[102] This 'expansion' is to be described by the OT theologian, who should attempt to demonstrate how the expansive development of human consciousness comes to a conclusion in the experience of the death and resurrection of Christ.[103]

What has happened in Gese's approach to the problem of Old and New Testaments is the reinforcement and further elaboration of a tendency already present in von Rad's OT theology, that is, the tendency to have theology replaced by a sort of phenomenology of tradition.[104] Gese expressly identifies 'revelation' and 'tradition process', and, consequently, theology must be identified with the description of this process. The inevitable result of such methodological confusion is a situation where allegedly *historical* analyses and investigations are at the same time, without any convincing reason, claimed to have a *theological* quality as statements about 'revelation'. There would seem to be little hope for either sound historical research or responsible theological analyses if this path is followed.

B. *The dialectical approach*
In 1948 Rudolf Bultmann made a significant contribution to the

debate on Old and New Testaments.[105] The first part of Bultmann's essay is devoted to demonstrating the invalidity of the sort of interpretation of OT prophecy represented by the NT writers, or rather, the impossibility of repeating their approach today. The early Christians were convinced that Christ and the Christian community were the fulfilment of the OT prophecies; the events foretold by the OT had now happened. Not only the prophetic writings in the strict sense, but the whole of the OT was seen as prophecy, although it was admitted that the predictions could only be properly understood after their fulfilment. Actually, according to Bultmann, the NT writers read into the OT texts something which was already known to them from elsewhere. Such an understanding of prophecy is both impossible today for historical reasons—since, obviously, it violates the OT texts—and theologically untenable because it aims at removing the offence from Christian preaching by showing that everything has been decided upon and prophesied long ago.[106] A different idea of prophecy and fulfilment is found in the nineteenth-century scholar Johann Christian Konrad von Hofmann, who sees the *history* of Israel, rather than the *words* of the OT, as prophecy. Naturally, Bultmann rejects the evolutionism of Hofmann, who was in this respect inspired by the philosophy of Hegel.[107] However, Bultmann follows Hofmann in regarding the history of Israel as prophecy. The decisive difference is that to Bultmann Christ is not the goal of history, but its eschatological end.[108] This thesis is developed by Bultmann through analyses of three central OT concepts, the Covenant, the Kingdom of God, and the People of God.[109] These concepts have one decisive feature in common. They cannot materialize within the realm of empirical history. Consequently, all the attempts made at linking their realization to the empirical Israelite people were destined to fail. The concepts were then given an eschatological significance, and in the NT they are interpreted in terms of a consequent eschatology. The New Covenant, the Kingdom of God, and the true People of God have now materialized in the Christian community which is *not* an empirical entity within the boundaries of this world.

The point Bultmann wants to make is that the history of Israel is prophecy, or 'promise', exactly because of its inherent inner contradictions, which spring from the attempt at realizing the eschatological in empirical, historical forms. 'In its very demonstration of this impossibility, the miscarriage of history actually amounts to a promise'.[110] The miscarriage of Israelite history demonstrates the impossibility of identifying the immanent history of man with the activity of God, it shows that man's own attempted way to salvation always leads to miscarriage. 'There is nothing which can count as promise to man other than the miscarriage of *his* way, and the recognition that it is impossible to gain direct access to God in his history within the world and directly to identify his history within the world with God's activity'.[111] But man's failure is only recognized as a promise when the fulfilment is there, when the possibility of a new existence is given in Christ to man who understands that his situation is hopeless.[112]

With this interpretation Bultmann wants to follow Paul's understanding of the law, which is both the good and holy will of God, and—when used by man as a way to salvation—leads to miscarriage.[113] Through this consideration Bultmann also attempts to determine the theological relevance of the OT promise. Faith always needs to be reminded of the law as the false way to salvation. Accordingly, faith needs to look back upon the history of Israel to be reminded that the state of justification presupposes the miscarriage of man. 'Thus faith, to be a really justifying faith, must constantly contain within itself the way of the law as something which has been overcome; it must also, in order to be an eschatological attitude, constantly contain within itself the attempt to identify what happens in the secular sphere with what happens eschatologically, as something which has been overcome'.[114]

Friedrich Baumgärtel's approach to the problem of Old and New Testaments rests on certain presuppositions which are frequently explained in his works. Baumgärtel's point of departure is his conviction that the theological relevance of OT texts is inseparably linked to their ability to grasp the Christian reader, to involve his person existentially. This ability of the texts Baumgärtel often calls their 'power' ('Mächtigkeit'). The relevance of the OT for the preaching of the Church is a main theme for Baumgärtel, whose interest in pastoral theology is evident from numerous passages in his writings. These two presuppositions are combined with a third. The results of historical-critical research are to be acknowledged without limitations. Baumgärtel is constantly on the watch against any tendency to neglect historical criticism.

We may begin by addressing the last point. It is a main concern of Baumgärtel that the religion-historical relativity of the OT be taken seriously. Under no circumstances should the distance between the

OT and Christianity be overlooked. The OT is a collection of religion-historical documents bearing witness to a religion different from the Christian religion. 'From the perspective of our contemporary thinking about the hermeneutical question the fact cannot be eliminated that the Old Testament is a witness from a religion outside the gospel and therefore from a religion strange to us. Viewed historically, it has another place than the Christian religion.'[115]

This does not mean that, according to Baumgärtel, there is no connection between the OT and Christianity. The message of the NT is God's gift of salvation or the 'promise in Christ' (Eph. 3.6), which is the realization of the OT promise.[116] In fact, it is striking that the NT uses the word 'promise', meaning in itself something still to be fulfilled, to designate salvation actual and present. The reason, Baumgärtel argues, is that the NT writers wanted to stress exactly this connection with the OT. That which had been promised to Israel under the Old Covenant had now become real in Christ.[117]

'Promise', in other words, is the motif which unites the Old Testament and the New. The NT 'promise in Christ' contains in itself the promise of the Old Covenant.[118] The OT promise has become real, actual, present in Christ.[119] However, this does not imply that Old and New Testaments interpret the 'promise' in identical ways. The NT 'promise in Christ' is characterized by what Baumgärtel calls its 'factuality'. Here salvation becomes real by being proclaimed. For the believer, God's promise materializes when he hears the gospel in faith.[120] The promise in Christ means justice, and eternal life, and thus it forms the ground which carries the believer's existence.[121] This is possible only because the promise is at the same time a judgment of man's sin. 'The promise in Christ becomes factual to me only in penitence'.[122]

Now the OT also knows of 'promises' even though it has no specific theological term.[123] The OT tells of divine promises given to individuals or to the people of Israel, promises of numerous offspring, of inheriting the land, of victory against enemies, and so forth— promises which are fulfilled during the course of history. Furthermore, we hear of conditional promises which are only fulfilled if the people obey the law, and, finally, there are the promises uttered by the prophets, which are inseparably linked to the expectation of certain future events. Common to all the OT promises is their intimate relation to Israel as a national entity and to the realm of terrestrial life. In this way their content is different from that of the NT promise, and, consequently, the OT promises are incapable of sustaining *our* lives, as they sustained the life of ancient Israel. What unites the OT promises and the 'promise in Christ' of the NT is their common 'ground', which Baumgärtel finds in God's revelation out of sovereign grace, as it is expressed in his covenant with Israel.[124] The OT understands the God of promise as the free and sovereign giver who approaches his people as Lord. This understanding grows out of faith in the covenant, or, as Baumgärtel says, of faith in the words 'I will be your God, and you shall be my people'. 'Then, after all, the promise in Christ in which even we Christians understand God as the one who gives out of his free will, as the one who as the Lord wants to draw us into his communion, is in continuity with the *ground* of all promises in the OT, with the *fundamental promise to Israel, — "I am the Lord thy God"*.'[125]

This 'fundamental promise' ('Grundverheissung') carries all the OT promises, and, at the same time, it motivates the threat of God's wrath, which is always present as 'the other side' of the promise, a threat which is occasioned by the continual disobedience of the Israelite people. This 'fundamental promise' has been fulfilled in the New Covenant. The OT itself, however, expected the 'fundamental promise' to come true in an entirely different way, since its expectations were determined by the limitations of OT religion. Here Baumgärtel insists on a very important distinction. His viewpoint is most clearly expressed when he deals with the promises and expectations of the OT prophets. It is crucial to Baumgärtel that 'promise' ('Verheissung') and 'prediction' ('Weissagung') be properly distinguished. God's absolute promise is something very different from the prophets' predictions of particular events. These predictions are aimed at explaining how God's promise and judgment are soon to come true. However, they are bound to the prophets' relative insight into history, and, consequently, liable to mistakes and illusions. Actually, the 'fundamental promise' was *not* fulfilled immediately after the national collapse of Israel in the way the prophets had predicted.[126] By linking the realization of God's absolute promise to the relative course of historical events the prophets made the promise relevant and meaningful to the Israelite people. But at the same time they contributed to bringing about the greatest catastrophe that ever befell a people. When God's fundamental promise *did* come true, this people crucified the one in whom the promise had materialized. For his appearance and his claims could not be brought into harmony with the predictions of the prophets.[127] Against this background it would seem obvious that only the absolute promise can be theologically relevant, and not the relative ideas about its realization found in the OT. However, as we shall soon see, Baumgärtel has more to say on this matter.

It is characteristic of Baumgärtel that in establishing the theological relevance of the OT texts he focuses on the question of their 'power' for the Christian reader or, as Baumgärtel prefers to phrase it, for the person who has been existentially grasped by the gospel. 'The Old Testament Word is to be understood as gospel, i.e., it must be made clear that, as conditioned Word outside the gospel, it is powerful for us, the active power of God for us; it is a witness which encounters and meets us in our existence together and as one with the evangelical witness'.[128]

Now, according to Baumgärtel, being grasped by the gospel, or by the 'promise in Christ' necessarily involves a certain kind of experience, which Baumgärtel describes in the following way. 'God exists, he is manifest as supreme power that encounters us as personal will in our brokenness, in order to draw us into his communion'.[129] And this 'fundamental experience' of the gospel is identical with the 'fundamental experience' of the OT. In fact, this identity is the true sense of Baumgärtel's statement that the 'fundamental promise' of the OT has come true in Christ.[130] '"I am the *Lord* thy God, I am the Lord *thy* God"—on that rests the old covenant, and that is the promise which comes with the old covenant. In this same fundamental experience, and in the evangelical knowledge through faith that the fundamental promise of the old covenant has been realized in Jesus Christ, is anchored the affinity of the Christian faith to the Old Testament Word'.[131] For Baumgärtel, this also motivates the existential relevance of the OT to Christian readers. The experience of the OT is their own experience, and in this sense the word of the OT is present and powerful as the word of God to them.[132]

What, then, becomes of the conditioned and relative contents of the OT with all those traits and features which, in Baumgärtel's opinion, reveal the limitations of a non-Christian religion? The answer that Baumgärtel offers involves a double aspect. In principle the OT is surpassed in this respect, it has—and for Baumgärtel this means the same thing—no 'power' in relation to the Christian.[133] But then Baumgärtel introduces another viewpoint. As a matter of fact, Christians are always striving to resist the gospel, and thus they remain bound to those very limitations which characterize the religion of the OT. Thus in reality their situation is the same as that of Israelite people. So, after all, the OT word does gain 'power' over them exactly in its conditioned and relative character. For Christians, this 'power' necessarily turns into a judgment since it reveals that their situation is, in fact, still the situation of humanity *before* the gospel, and not, as it should be, that of humanity *under* the gospel.[134]

But the OT texts do not only judge Christians in this way, they also provide them with invaluable consolation. For they are allowed to hear the OT word as a word which has already been overcome. 'But in experiencing the judging power of the Old Testament witness we also experience at the same time and under the same Old Testament Word the gracious and comforting knowledge that these are words *outside* the gospel, words from limited and restricted circumstances, and Christ has long since released us from them'.[135] So, for Christians, the 'conditioned' witness of the OT is both judgment and consolation, judgment because they have to recognize their own situation and their own way of thinking in the OT texts, and consolation because they can hear this witness as the *old* witness which, as such, *has* been overcome in Christ.

In this manner the OT becomes theologically relevant in its conditioned relativity. It is a word that has been overcome through the gospel, and yet it remains powerful and present, and constantly needs to be overcome again. Probably the best summary of Baumgärtel's hermeneutical intentions is found in some words of his own.

> The whole gravity of the contemporary problem concerning the Old Testament comes from the fact that the historical-critical research implicit in our contemporary historical thinking has sharply recognized the Old Testament as the witness of a religion outside the gospel. It almost seems as if many have not even comprehended that today we must first lose the Old Testament completely, i.e., comprehend it in its self-understanding as completely separate from the New Testament and in no way 'justified' through the gospel!—in order to win it back again at all. The problem concerning this winning it back again is the hermeneutical problem today.[136]

Viewed as a whole, Baumgärtel's approach makes a very coherent impression, once the basic presuppositions are taken into consideration. In a certain sense, it may be appropriate to speak of Baumgärtel as a 'liberal theologian'. The fact that his point of departure lies within the realm of psychology, and the eminent importance he ascribes to history of religion, are hints in this direction. At the same time, however, Baumgärtel is obviously highly conscious of his Lutheran confession. His preferred systematic authorities are the markedly confessional Lutheran theologians Werner Elert and Paul Althaus.[137] And it is evident that the model for Baumgärtel's understanding of the relevance of the 'conditioned' witness of the OT is derived from the interpretation of the law in Lutheran tradition. The Christian, being *simul justus et peccator*, constantly needs the accusing word of the law as a 'schoolmaster to bring us unto Christ' (Gal. 3.24).[138]

However, it cannot be overlooked that there are some serious problems involved in Baumgärtel's programme. One difficulty concerns his fundamental thesis that the OT bears witness to a 'non-Christian' religion. Here it should be noted that 'Christian' (or 'evangelical', to use one of Baumgärtel's favourite synonyms) may have at least two different meanings. As a *religion-historical* term 'Christian' is used to designate what is proper to the 'Christian religion' as a historical phenomenon. Naturally, all things dating from before the origin of this historical phenomenon must from a religion-historical point of view be labelled 'non-Christian'. The OT falls under this category, but so does, for example, the teaching of Jesus, since the 'Christian religion' as a historical phenomenon did not arise until after his death. In other words, to the extent that the gospels give an authentic picture of the teaching of Jesus they too bear witness to a 'non-Christian' religion. In this religion-historical perspective they are 'Christian' documents only in so far as they have been decisively marked by the religion of the primitive Church. But then, 'Christian' may also be used as a *theological* term to denote things legitimate and valid in the Christian Church. And when the word is employed in this way, it is obvious that categories of time *per se* cannot be decisive. When Baumgärtel speaks of the OT as bearing witness to a 'non-Christian' religion, there can be little doubt that he intends to make a religion-historical statement. According to Baumgärtel, it is a 'fact, derived from study of the history of religion, that the Old Testament is a witness out of a non-Christian religion'.[139] Nevertheless, this interpretation of 'non-Christian' as a religion-historical term is not consistently maintained. This becomes obvious from the fact that Baumgärtel regards things 'Christian' as in some sense exempt from religion-historical study. In one place he writes:

> The Old Testament Word is the active Word of God, the power of God to the Old Testament and New Testament man alike. However, it can have power for the evangelical man as Old Testament Word only as a witness which is conditioned by historical and religious development and which moves outside the gospel in its self-understanding. It cannot have power for the evangelical man as evangelical Word, because it is not evangelical Word.[140]

This formulation can only mean that whatever is 'Christian' or 'evangelical'—as e.g. the 'evangelical Word'—is *not* 'conditioned by historical and religious development'. This, of course, is inconsistent, a slip from religion-historical into theological categories. Indeed, the slip is apparent from the very use of 'evangelical' ('evangelisch') with all its connotations as a synonym for 'Christian'. From a religion-historical point of view, both Old and New Testaments are collections of religion-historical documents, and, naturally, the NT is exactly as historically 'conditioned' as the OT. Religion-historical study may compare the religions of Old and New Testaments synchronically, assessing similarities and differences, or, alternatively, these religions may be analysed in a diachronic perspective allowing the historian to recognize historical continuity as well as discontinuity. Nothing of this amounts to theological statements. From a theological point of view Old and New Testaments are not regarded primarily as collections of religion-historical documents, but as the canon of the Church, as the normative basis for preaching the Christian gospel.

It would seem that, in a sense, the NT alone is canon in Baumgärtel's conception. However, this is obviously not in harmony with his own intentions.[141] It cannot be denied, though, that there is a fundamental obscurity involved in the confusion of religion-historical and theological perspectives. Thus, when Baumgärtel stresses the 'limitations' of OT religion, he certainly intends to state *religion-historical* facts. Actually, it is evident that his statements contain an implicit *theological* judgment.

Another difficulty is Baumgärtel's rather idiosyncratic use of the Lutheran concepts of law and gospel. In Luther's theology there is no schematic connection between the theological categories law and gospel on the one hand and the literary *corpora* OT and NT on the other. Law and gospel are not primarily hermeneutical principles in biblical exegesis—although they are this too—but rather what one might call 'categories of reality'. Law and gospel are the alternative possibilities, diametrically opposed, for the relationship between God and man, and, consequently, for man's relations to reality. In spite of his indisputable deep familiarity with Lutheran tradition, Baumgärtel's use of the dialectics of law and gospel as a hermeneutical scheme must be characterized as a formalistic distortion.

C. *The problem of 'salvation history'*

As already mentioned, Gerhard von Rad regards it as an essential quality of Israel's faith that it has its foundation in Yahweh's acts in history. In a section on the origins of Hebrew ideas of history[142] in the second volume of von Rad's OT theology, we are told how the way the Israelites viewed Yahweh's saving acts underwent a highly significant historical development. At first the individual historical traditions (patriarchal traditions, exodus traditions, settlement traditions) were mutually independent, and associated with the cults of various local shrines. Then, however, at some early stage, they were combined to a unified whole, and from then on the *series* of historical events as such came to be regarded more and more as the constitutive *raison d'être* of the Israelite people. According to von Rad, the result of this process can be seen from the 'creeds', which are in fact nothing but summaries of salvation history. In this conception of 'salvation history'—which, von Rad believes, was in essentials already there in the period of the judges—Israel departed radically from its ancient Near Eastern environment. In Israel, history came to be viewed as a linear movement, as opposed to the various cyclic conceptions of her neighbouring peoples.[143]

Thus, the idea of 'salvation history' is the result—unique from the point of view of cultural and religious history—of a development of tradition within Israel. Originally disparate historical traditions were unified into a series of successive events, and the importance assigned to each of these events now became inseparable from the place of that event within the series. Now the question arises how 'salvation history' and history of tradition are interrelated, if 'salvation history' or the idea of 'salvation history' is a product of the particular Israelite history of religion. If 'salvation history' is in some sense the result of the history of tradition, what becomes of the allegedly indispensable foundation in historical facts, which, according to von Rad, is essential to Israelite faith? Or is the history of tradition itself to be regarded as a part of 'salvation history'? Or is history of tradition perhaps even identical with 'salvation history' in the proper sense?

Von Rad is certainly intensely aware of these problems, although he prefers to pose the fundamental question in somewhat different terms. Israelite faith rests on divine acts in history, which are definitely regarded by Israel as 'historical facts' ('Geschichtstatsachen'). However, the picture of Israel's history drawn by the OT does not correspond with the results of modern critical scholarship. Consequently, two diverging conceptions are facing one another. On the one hand, we have the critical reconstruction of Israel's history, and on the other the picture which Israel herself drew of her own history, a picture which is determined in its entirety by Israel's belief in Yahweh, and has the character of 'confession'. Von Rad speaks with preference of the 'kerygmatic' picture of Israel's history. These two 'pictures' are the results of entirely different endeavours. One is the product of a rational quest for things verifiable, the other is derived from a confessional involvement in history.[144] This double aspect presents the OT theologian with an urgent problem. 'The fact that these two views of Israel's history are so divergent is one of the most serious burdens imposed today upon Biblical scholarship'.[145]

The problem itself seems to have two different aspects. The first aspect concerns the inevitable divergence in the way particular historical events and developments are regarded. In this connection von Rad emphasizes that the Israelite view of history is important in its own right, and must be interpreted accordingly. The 'confessional' representation of history has its own rules and laws, and above all its modes of expression show a high degree of affinity to those of poetry. This does not mean, though, that it is not founded in actual historical experience, but the historical events are here experienced and expressed with a maximal intensity, and in a condensed form which renders any separation of fact and interpretation impossible.[146]

But secondly, von Rad also speaks in more general terms of the divergence between modern historical criticism and ancient Israelite views of history. In an article in 1963 he writes:

> Only where Yahweh had revealed himself with his deeds and his word was there history for Israel. And at this point the conflict with the modern view of history was bound to arise, sooner or later. For the modern view is perfectly capable of drawing a picture of history

without God. The supposition of divine action in history is very
difficult from a modern viewpoint. In the modern picture of history
God is much rather an alien.[147]

Here contradictory ideas of history, its causes and motives, are
opposed. Does this mean that we have to do with an insoluble
conflict? Are we left with the choice between a history with God and
a history without him? And is it von Rad's suggestion that the OT
theologian should then choose the former alternative which would
seem to imply the rejection of historical criticism in principle?
Indeed, von Rad does not give us a totally unambiguous answer,[148]
although certain statements may sound as if he would deny in
principle the adequacy of historical criticism in relation to the task of
understanding the picture of history drawn by the OT. Such a
consequence, however, is explicitly rejected by von Rad elsewhere.
He is not concerned with finding a new method, but rather with
having the historical-critical method handled with greater flexibility
and in more careful adaptation to the subject matter.[149] Nevertheless
it is evident that von Rad would like somehow to limit the realm of
historical criticism, in order to allow the OT to speak more freely for
itself.[150] In all probability, then, von Rad is to be interpreted in the
sense that the historical-critical and the confessional views of
Israelite history are both legitimate, although either view is able to
represent only a partial aspect of historical reality.[151]

Franz Hesse, whose criticism of von Rad's methodology has been
referred to above, sees in the discrepancy between the historical-
critical conception of Israel's history and Israel's own view, as
presented and lamented by von Rad, the symptom of a fundamental
confusion inherent in his theology.[152] This confusion, Hesse argues,
is due to the fact that von Rad, following a long tradition within OT
theology, is mistaken in the way he locates 'salvation history'.
According to Hesse, the idea of 'salvation history' means that the
history of Israel possesses a unique quality because God has spoken
and acted in this history in a unique manner.[153] However, since the
rise of historical criticism the divergence between factual history and
its presentation in the OT has become ever more evident. Against
this background, OT theologians have been inclined to ascribe the
qualities of 'salvation history' to the so-called 'biblical history', i.e.
the picture of history presented in the Bible, and not to the factual
'history of Israel', which was then left to be treated by non-
theological critical research.[154] As opposed to this trend, Hesse

suggests that the difficulty arising from the divergence between the OT view of history and factual history, as reconstructed through the methods of critical scholarship, may be overcome by making the very opposite choice. The qualities of 'salvation history', he argues, must be ascribed to factual history. Only where something has actually taken place is it possible to speak of God's acts in history and thus of 'salvation history' in the proper sense.[155] 'Salvation history' is present, although hidden, within this 'real' or factual history, which can only be investigated by means of historical criticism. Consequently, the critical study of history becomes a proper theological task, though the particular quality assigned to the history of Israel as the 'salvation history' remains a statement of faith which as such cannot be proven by theology.[156]

In other words, Hesse accepts von Rad's presupposition that there is an inevitable tension between the historical-critical and the 'kerygmatic' conceptions of history, although for theological reasons Hesse feels compelled to make the opposite choice. An entirely different line is adopted by Rolf Rendtorff, who attempts to develop further the intentions found in von Rad's work, assuming, however, that this tension may be eliminated.[157] Rendtorff's main thesis is the inseparability of tradition and history. Using the OT traditions about Abraham as an example, Rendtorff argues that it is impossible through critical research to establish any facts concerning the life and time of Abraham. Historically, it is only possible to trace and reconstruct some of the stages and transitions in the complex process of tradition.[158] The continuous transformations involved in this process render it equally impossible to point to any one particular 'kerygmatic' picture of the Abraham tradition.[159] So irrespective of whether we set out to search for 'factual history' or to identify a historical *kerygma*, we are inevitably faced with the history of tradition.[160] And in fact, Rendtorff proceeds, it is true of the entire history of Israel that the development and transmission of traditions are of the utmost importance as an integral part of this history. Indeed, as far as the oldest history is concerned the traditions are often all the historian can possibly get hold of.[161]

Now the point Rendtorff wants to make is that a distinction between history and tradition, or between fact and interpretation, is not only impossible for practical purposes, but that it is not in the least desirable either. Actually, this distinction is derived from a philosophically untenable idea of what history is.[162] Theologically, the impossibility of separating history from tradition means that the acts of God must be seen as taking place in the very unity of history and tradition. In other words, 'salvation history' has to comprise the whole of history, including the history of tradition.[163] And consequently, the disciplines 'history of Israel', 'history of OT traditions', and 'OT theology' should no longer be distinguished in principle, since they must all deal with God's acts in history in this comprehensive sense.[164]

At this point Rendtorff criticizes von Rad for not having carried out his own intentions with sufficient consistency. OT theology ought to align itself not only with OT introduction but even with the history of Israel. According to Rendtorff, the fact that von Rad is left with the unsolved problem of two conflicting conceptions of history indicates that he has not quite managed to disentangle himself from the influence of conventional viewpoints on history. The domain of historical criticism should not be restricted, Rendtorff argues; rather should the methods of historical criticism be developed and refined in a way that would enable it to 'comprise the whole of history in its manifoldness'. This, admittedly, implies that the conventional version of 'historical-critical research' has to be criticized.[165] Such viewpoints make it evident that Rendtorff belongs to the circle of Wolfhart Pannenberg.

The criticisms of both Rendtorff and Hesse point to a problem unsolved in von Rad's OT theology. How are tradition and history interrelated? And how is 'salvation history' to be located in this context? The reason why this problem is not solved in a satisfactory manner here is undoubtedly to be sought in the fundamental tension within von Rad's theology between the perspective of *kerygma* and that of salvation history. On the one hand he emphasizes the 'kerygmatic' character of the OT texts, the fact that they address the reader directly, not to convey objective information, but in order to be heard as confession and proclamation with the ultimate intention of leading the hearer to faith. The affinity of these ideas with Bultmann's approach to the proclamation of Christ in NT texts is obvious.[166] In this perspective all emphasis is placed on the kerygmatic intention of the texts, rather than on their 'objective' relation to facts of history. On the other hand von Rad also wants to stress the historical foundation of Israelite faith, a faith which he describes as being based on 'historical facts' ('Geschichtstatsachen').

It is obvious that Rendtorff and Pannenberg have grasped the latter tendency, that of 'salvation history', and attempted to carry it through to the bitter end, neglecting totally and deliberately the 'kerygmatic' tendency. Whether they can justly claim to be von Rad's true followers, and whether they are right in declaring him the father of the 'revelation as history' theology, remains an open question. In any case their endeavour is a one-sided 'rationalization' of von Rad's theology. It is possible, of course, that this was in fact von Rad's true intention.[167] However, von Rad himself remains inconsistent because the perspectives of kerygma and of salvation history cannot be reconciled. Indeed, this inconsistency may also be viewed as a sign of von Rad's theological concern: he remained troubled by the fundamental problems, and was unable to deal with them in a fixed, comprehensive schema.

At first glance it may seem to be a surprising fact that even Friedrich Baumgärtel is able to find a place for the notion of 'salvation history' within his 'dialectical' view of the relationship between OT and NT. Nevertheless, Baumgärtel has written an entire essay on OT events as salvation history[168], and the contents of that essay may serve to illustrate his general view in an instructive manner.

Baumgärtel's point of departure is the thesis that in a Christian perspective 'salvation history' is identical with the historical event of Jesus Christ, the event in which salvation is given to the believer. 'Salvation history' in the Christian sense is the event summarized in the sentence 'The Word became Flesh', in so far as this event becomes relevant to humanity in faith.[169] The external course of events can never in itself possess the quality of 'salvation history'.[170]

First and foremost, then, salvation history is the history of Jesus Christ. However, this history contains within itself the salvation history of the OT. By this Baumgärtel means that the Christological event is the realization of God's promise. The OT history can only be salvation history in so far as it is related to the Christ-event.[171] At this point, though, Baumgärtel introduces one of his favourite distinctions. The events related in the OT are 'salvation history' in one sense to ancient Israel and in another sense to present-day theology. For Israel 'salvation history' meant that God's fundamental promise in its double aspect of grace and demand determined the people's history. This history possessed the double character of 'salvation history' and 'history of judgment' ('Unheilsgeschichte'). To clarify how 'salvation history' is understood in the OT texts is a historical task.[172] However, in a theological perspective—and for Baumgärtel this always means in a Christian perspective—the events of the OT can only be 'salvation history' when they are made existentially relevant for Christians in relation to the gospel, and when they are experienced by them as judgment and comfort.[173] This does not mean that Baumgärtel wants to assign some sort of second meaning to the testimony of the OT. Just as the OT word was 'powerful' to OT humanity, so can it be existentially relevant for the Christian.[174] Here again we encounter Baumgärtel's understanding of the OT as judgment and consolation in its historically conditioned relativity.

We have mentioned Franz Hesse's criticism of von Rad, and his attempt at connecting the idea of 'salvation history' with the factual history of Israel as reconstructed by critical scholarship. In 1966 this was still Hesse's position.[175] However, in 1971, in a monograph bearing the significant title *Abschied von der Heilsgeschichte* ('A Farewell to Salvation History') he pleads for dispensing altogether with this theological notion.[176]

Initially Hesse attempts to define or at least to describe with some exactitude the meaning of 'salvation history', a notion which, he complains, has often been used by theological writers in a rather careless and imprecise manner. The idea of 'salvation history' implies an intimate relationship between salvation and the course of history. Either, salvation is conceived of as being in some sense *present* within history, or salvation is the *goal* of history, in which case 'salvation history' is in a positive or negative manner the *preparation* for salvation.[177]

Hesse then proceeds to investigate whether the history of Israel can be interpreted as 'salvation history' in any of these senses. To a remarkable degree he accepts von Rad's viewpoints concerning the early origins of a unique historical consciousness in ancient Israel.[178] However, he sees no possibility of understanding Israel's history as represented in the OT as a history in which salvation is present. According to the OT the saving acts of Yahweh are constantly interrupted and frustrated through the disobedience of the people, and the punishments Yahweh then has to inflict. Salvation remains something still to be expected.[179] The time of David and Solomon is the only episode which is possibly viewed by the OT as 'salvation history' in this sense.[180] The view that prevails in the OT sees the history of Israel as a history of judgment. Sometimes this highly pessimistic view is counterbalanced by the expectation of future salvation or by eschatological ideas; sometimes it is carried through without relief, leading to the conclusion that Israel's history is determined in its entirety by the people's guilt and Yahweh's punishment. According to Hesse, the latter viewpoint is that of the Deuteronomistic literature.[181]

Having shown that the OT allows no interpretation of Israel's history as 'salvation history' in the sense of a history in which salvation is present, Hesse turns to the NT. The question is now whether the history of Israel can be understood as a history which somehow prepares for the history of Jesus Christ. However, Hesse finds no trace of such a view in the NT writings. Neither the gospels nor Paul nor the non-Pauline epistles show any interest, Hesse claims, in a continuous OT 'salvation history'.[182] Still the idea might in itself be a theologically valid and necessary one. Hesse therefore proceeds to address the systematic question of whether it is legitimate to speak of a 'salvation history' with Jesus Christ as centre and the time of the OT as preparation.[183] This inevitably leads to the problem with which Hesse was already concerned in his criticism of von Rad, i.e. that of locating this hypothetical 'salvation history' in relation to factual history and to the history described by the biblical writers. Identifying the factual history of Israel with 'salvation history', which would mean assuming that the history of this particular people was in some special way affected and determined by the acts of God, is unacceptable to Hesse. The ideas of Israel's election and of God's intervention in history do not necessarily imply the notion of a continuous series of supernatural events. Furthermore, Israel's history in this sense cannot be univocally defined and isolated from history in general.[184] As for the 'biblical history', or the history which the writers of the OT and the NT describe, it remains a fiction which has never taken place in time and space, and, consequently, it cannot be identified with 'salvation history'.[185] Hesse's own earlier idea of 'salvation history' being invisibly present within the factual history of Israel is also rejected now. The decisive argument is that history as such cannot be the object of faith. Indeed faith may ascribe a certain meaning to historical events and to the course of history, but there can be no such thing as a historical continuity which is attainable to faith alone.[186]

In a final chapter entitled 'the question of continuity' Hesse addresses the entire problem once more.[187] According to Hesse, the concept of history implies the idea of continuity, and this must also be true of 'salvation history'. Now obviously the factual history of Israel can and must be conceived of as a continuous course of events, even if our lack of exact knowledge and information prevents us from reconstructing the continuity.[188] But as far as acts of God are concerned, it is their essential characteristic that they lack causality and finality, and consequently, they cannot be comprised within historical continuity. God's activity, Hesse states, is not continuous but contingent.[189] It follows that there can be no question of a 'salvation history' within the factual history of Israel. Direct, miraculous divine intervention would destroy the continuity. Naturally, historical events may always be interpreted as determined by the will of God. Such an interpretation, however, is applicable to any event of history, and cannot be used to ascribe a particular quality to the history of Israel.[190]

Actually, it is evident that divine miracles which wreck the continuity of history are unacceptable to Hesse. The miraculous events related in the OT are labelled 'mythical' and unhistorical.[191] And even God's saving act in Jesus Christ cannot be claimed to surpass historical continuity. In itself the history of Jesus forms a part of immanent history. Admittedly, the quality of Jesus Christ as saviour is exempt from historical calculations, but it does not, as it were, break into history either. According to Hesse, the unique importance of Christ is in a sense assigned to him from outside. God has chosen to communicate salvation through the gospel of Christ, and his significance is only attainable to faith. In the preaching of the Church the importance of Christ is proclaimed as a marvel, and it cannot be prepared for through a 'salvation history'. On the contrary, Christ delivers man from history, for in history man is always out to conquer his life, and to constitute himself as a master of it.[192]

The notion of 'salvation history', Hesse concludes, is theologically untenable; it ought to be dropped, and the sooner the better.[193]

It is obvious that Hesse's viewpoints are anything but original. In fact I dealt with his book in some detail exactly because he is to a high degree representative of the views held by the 'existentialist' theologians. It is no surprise, therefore, to find that Hesse quotes prominent advocates of this school, such as Ernst Fuchs and Günter Klein, as authorities.[194] The decisive weakness of the 'existentialist' position is also clearly exhibited in Hesse's work. The remission of sins proclaimed in the preaching of the Church seems to have but the slenderest relation to the historical Christ. Ultimately, the historical reference tends to lose all significance. Hesse is definitely right in pleading for a more accurate use of the term 'salvation history'. However, it is hardly advisable to dispense with this notion altogether, as he suggests. After all, the very fact that it is used in so many different theological conceptions would seem to indicate that it contains aspects of importance for theology.

4. *The Problem of 'Canon'*

The concept of 'canon' and the problems and questions it occasions played no special part in the OT debate of the 1950s. Very probably, this had to do with the fact that the canonical authority of Scripture was widely and commonly recognized, indeed, more or less regarded as an axiom, in the theological climate of that period. Naturally, this is a very general claim. Once we begin to examine the ways in which various theologians understood the implications of scriptural authority, a much more complicated picture emerges. However, Protestant theologians of the post-war period rarely questioned the principle of scriptural authority as such. Rather, they would generally acknowledge that theological exegesis presupposed the normative status of Scripture with regard to the preaching of the Church. Undoubtedly this reverence for the authority of Scripture must be seen partly as a result of Barthian influence, in a broad sense, and partly as an outcome of the 'Church conflict' in Germany and the particular theological climate it created.

This is not to say that the problem of canon was of no importance. Only, the problem was usually active in indirect ways, rather than being a theme of explicit debate. Occasionally, however, the question of 'canon' did occur more overtly in the discussion, as, for example, in Baumgärtel's criticism of von Rad for lacking a clear concept of 'revelation'.[195] Furthermore, it is obvious that the 'canonical' function of the OT as basis for the preaching of the Church was of central importance in the hermeneutical endeavours of the *Biblischer Kommentar* group. And, as we have seen, the canonical authority of the OT was highly influential in von Rad's theology. In a sense, von Rad regards the 'testimony' of the OT as directly authoritative, although the precise nature and implications of this authority are not made the subject of explicit theological reflection.[196]

In the 1970s 'canon' and the questions related to that concept were given a prominent place on the agenda of theological debate.

Probably the most noticeable attempt at making 'canon' the key concept in biblical theology is found in the work of Brevard S. Childs. In his book *Biblical Theology in Crisis* (1970) the programme is sketched in the following way.

> As a fresh alternative, we would like to defend the thesis that the canon of the Christian church is the most appropriate context from which to do Biblical Theology.[197]

By 'context' Childs means in a broad and comprehensive sense the environment within which the biblical texts are interpreted, and to which they are related by the exegete.[198] When the canonical status of the Bible is declared the proper context for doing biblical theology, it means that the function of the Bible as a normative vehicle for divine revelation in the Christian Church is to be taken seriously.[199] In itself, however, the canonicity of Scripture remains a statement of faith, which as such cannot be demonstrated.[200] For Childs, interpreting the Bible within the context of the canon implies that the Old Testament and the New are to be exegetically interrelated, although no specific rules can be established for this exegetical procedure in individual cases. Both OT and NT texts should be read in relation to their own particular historical situation, but not in isolation.[201]

In his OT introduction Childs has attempted to carry out this programme on a larger scale, whilst at the same time both clarifying and elaborating his position.[202] Here Childs relates his exegetical principles to certain viewpoints on the development of the OT literature. This development is interpreted as a 'canonical process', the origins of which can be traced back to the oldest traditions of Israel. The 'canonical history' of the OT is not identical with the history of Israelite literature in a broader sense, although the two are closely connected and at times inseparable for all practical purposes.[203] The canon is the result of a process which had its own laws, determined by the use of traditions within a religious community.

> Beginning in the pre-exilic period, but increasing in significance in the post-exilic era, a force was unleashed by Israel's religious use of her traditions which exerted an influence on the shaping of the literature as it was selected, collected and ordered.[204]

One characteristic feature of this 'canonical history' is the scrupulous way in which the persons involved, the redactors and editors of the 'canonical' OT, have safeguarded their anonymity. Moreover, the original differences between various sociological and historical groups within ancient Israel were consciously blurred, as the Jewish community found its identity in its relation to 'canonical' literature. 'Israel defined itself in terms of a book!'[205]

From this idea of a 'canonical process' behind the OT, Childs is able to draw certain conclusions regarding the task of OT exegesis. One implication is that any quest for political, social, or economical motives behind the biblical texts is impermissible or at any rate highly dubious.

> It is constitutive of Israel's history that the literature formed the identity of the religious community which in turn shaped the literature. This fundamental dialectic which lies at the heart of the canonical process is lost when the critical Introduction assumes that a historically referential reading of the Old Testament is the key to its interpretation. It assumes the determining force on every biblical text to be political, social or economic factors which it seeks to establish in disregard of the religious dynamic of the canon.[206]

Furthermore, the 'canonical' approach means that the exegete has to ascribe a decisive significance to the final form of the texts. For in its definitive form the biblical text reflects a 'history of revelation', or an 'encounter between God and Israel', and the final shape of the text exercises a critically normative function over against earlier stages. 'Canonical' exegesis acknowledges and defends this normative authority of the final 'canonical' form of the texts.[207] This is true of larger and smaller literary units alike. Thus, Childs argues, the canonical form of the Book of Isaiah implies that the message of Second Isaiah is given a new perspective. Through their separation from the particular historical situation in which they originally belonged, that is, the Babylonian exile, his prophecies have been given a new 'eschatological' significance, which is valid for all times.[208]

With or without Childs' own consent his programme has been labelled 'canonical criticism' in the Anglo-American theological world. Doubtlessly, its most conspicuous feature is the emphasis on the absolute authority of the final 'canonical' form of the Bible as a whole and of the individual biblical books and texts.

In some of his recent works James Barr has launched a severe criticism of Childs's programme.[209] A point of fundamental importance is the ambiguity, demonstrated by Barr, in Childs's use of the terms 'canon' and 'canonical'. According to Barr, the original and proper meaning of the word 'canon' is 'the list of books which together comprise holy scripture'.[210] In Childs's usage, though, 'canon' obviously means more than this. Childs employs the term 'canonical' to denote the final shape of an individual biblical book or text, and, moreover, in Childs's works 'canon' comes to mean a certain interpretative perspective, namely the so-called 'holistic' approach to the biblical texts.[211] Evidently it is essential to Childs's position that all these aspects of 'canon' belong together. This, however, is exactly what Barr tries to show is erroneous. In fact, he argues, these ideas of 'canon' reflect diverging and, indeed, partly conflicting tendencies. The final form of the biblical book is the result of a literary process. However, from a historical point of view, the canonization of these books as Holy Scripture meant that the literary genre of each individual book was disregarded. Through canonization the texts came to be regarded as divinely inspired even down to their smallest parts, and theological arguments could now be based upon individual passages regardless of their literary context. In other words, the establishment of the 'canon' in this sense led to a 'massive decontextualization', and the effect was neglect of the final literary shape of the biblical books, rather than appreciation of it.[212]

Barr also criticizes the picture drawn by Childs of a 'canonical process' behind the OT. The very notion of a 'canonization', Barr points out, is derived from the history of the Christian Church, and it is doubtful whether it is at all relevant to the history of the OT writings. The OT was a national literature with an intrinsic traditional authority, and it is hardly possible to show that there was at any time much interest in distinguishing 'canonical' books from heretical ones.[213] Indeed, there may well be said to have existed a sort of 'pre-canon', i.e. a 'core of central and agreed tradition', which from a very early stage in the history of Israel exercised functions similar to those of the later scriptural canon. In that case, though, the only possible means by which the contents of this 'pre-canon' may be established is historical reconstruction—which means that the exclusive emphasis on the final shape of the biblical canon has to be given up.[214]

In more general terms Barr points out that it is exactly the 'synchronic' reading of the biblical texts which leads the interpreter to include a historical perspective.[215] Earlier stages or strata in the texts are, if recognizable, legitimate parts of Scripture as well as the results of the final redaction.[216] Moreover, Barr thinks that the latest stages of both the Old Testament and the New are marked by unmistakable tendencies of decay and deterioration, and it is therefore in either case dubious to assign a particular authority to the people of the 'canonizing period'.[217]

The decisive error of 'canonical criticism', according to Barr, lies in its belief in the canon as a hermeneutical guide. To expect hermeneutical guidance from the canon as such is obviously an illusion.

> The canon does not tell us whether the Synoptic Gospels are to be understood in the light of John, or the reverse, or whether Paul is to be understood in the light of the Gospels or the reverse . . . On basic questions concerning the balance of biblical evidence, such as the question whether justification by faith is the kernel of the Gospel, or whether predestination is rightly considered as an architectonic theme, or whether the idea of creation is theologically derivative from redemption or not, the canon as such seems to tell us nothing.[218]

By taking refuge in the purely formal principle of 'canon' the adherents of 'canonical criticism' apparently obtain an indisputable and universally recognized vantage point. In reality, though, the problems of biblical theology cannot be solved by means of a formal principle.[219] A truly theological approach to the Bible necessarily involves the quest for the reality *behind* the texts, the reality to which the texts refer and bear witness.[220]

Barr's critical observations are well made. The 'canonical' programme of Childs ascribes an unwarrantable importance to the *formal* aspect of 'canon'. The final form of the biblical texts is given an absolute theological quality. This is all the more regrettable because it may in many instances be exegetically legitimate and fruitful to focus more than has usually been done hitherto on motives and intentions behind the latest redactional activity the texts have undergone. To insist on the absolute theological authority of the final result, however, means to exclude *a priori* any possibility that the redactors might have misunderstood or deliberately distorted the original and proper meaning of the texts they had before them. In other words this predominantly formal understanding of the canon leads to historically and exegetically unjustifiable procedures. This is not to say, though, that the status and function of the Bible as the canon of the Christian Church is unimportant for theological exegesis. Rather, the canonicity of Scripture should be seen in relation to the *contents* of the biblical books, and to their function in theology and preaching.

5. *The Problem of 'Biblical Theology'*

In order to avoid confusion, it may be useful to examine briefly the different ways in which the expression 'biblical theology' is used in Anglo-American and in continental terminology. In the English-speaking countries the term has several meanings. Firstly, as in continental tradition, 'biblical theology' means a theological discipline which analyses and explains main themes and common trends in the biblical literature. Secondly, 'biblical theology' is used in a broader sense, more or less as a synonym for 'biblical exegesis'. Under the heading 'biblical theology' a university lecture programme may include all academic instruction covering the fields of Old and New Testament studies. And thirdly, 'Biblical Theology' is the commonly accepted name of a certain theological movement with a strong 'biblical' and partly 'neo-orthodox' orientation, which more or less dominated American biblical studies during the first part of the post-war period.

In the following, however, 'biblical theology' is used in accordance with continental terminology. Here the term designates a branch of theological studies, which, as a special discipline, goes back to the seventeenth century;[221] the purpose and methods of this discipline were later programmatically formulated by Johann Philipp Gabler in his famous inaugural lecture from 1787.[222] Gabler's main point is that 'biblical theology' is a historical discipline which has to be carefully distinguished from dogmatic theology. The development since Gabler has tended to make 'biblical theology' a merely formal common name of the mutually independent disciplines 'OT theology' and 'NT theology'.

'Biblical theology' has been a much debated theme during most of the post-war era, although it is hardly to be denied that interest has increased in recent years. In 1955 Gerhard Ebeling wrote an essay on the subject which remains worthwhile reading.[223] Initially, Ebeling points to the ambiguity inherent in the term itself. Does 'biblical theology' mean 'the theology contained in the Bible', or 'theology in accordance with the Bible'? In the former case, we have to do with a historical concept, and in the latter with a normative concept.[224] Actually, the whole problem of biblical theology is in a certain sense rooted in this ambiguity.

In order to clarify this problem, Ebeling draws a rough, yet instructive sketch of the history of the concept 'biblical theology'. The background, which made such a notion possible, is the *sola Scriptura* emphasis of the Reformation, although no thorough methodological reflection on this principle is found in the theology of the Reformers themselves.[225] The expression 'biblical theology' emerged in the seventeenth century as a slogan used by the early Pietist movement in its criticism of Protestant Orthodoxy. At the same time, 'biblical theology' came to be used as the name of a theological subsidiary discipline with the task of collecting and accounting for the *dicta probantia* or the scriptural foundation of dogmatics.[226] Then, in the Enlightenment period 'biblical theology' became an alternative dogmatic theology, which rivalled the position of traditional dogmatics.[227] In this manner biblical theology gains a remarkably ambiguous identity. As a historical discipline biblical theology is very conscious of its independence from dogmatics. At the same time, however, biblical theology is just as conscious of exercising a critical and normative function over against dogmatics. And lastly, biblical theology itself remains deeply influenced by dogmatic motives.[228] The history of biblical theology has, Ebeling argues, rendered the very idea of a 'biblical theology' problematic. The unity of the Bible seems to dissolve completely when consequent historical viewpoints are applied, and the idea of an authoritative canon seems to lose its meaning. Moreover, the traditional use of the term 'theology' to denote the contents of the Bible has been shown to be at least very dubious.[229]

Ebeling focuses on the last point, and adds some reflections which are meant to provide the ground for establishing a proper meaning of 'biblical theology'. Although the greater part of the Bible does not contain 'theology' in the strict sense its contents are capable of, and, indeed, require, theological explication. In the Bible itself, traces of such explication can be found e.g. in the Pauline Epistles and in the Fourth Gospel. 'Biblical theology', then, can be defined as the 'scientific explication' of what the OT and the NT contain.[230] First and foremost, Ebeling has in mind the separate disciplines of OT theology and NT theology. Nevertheless, he is also able to envisage a comprehensive biblical theology, the task of which he describes in the following way.

> In 'Biblical theology' the theologian who devotes himself specially to studying the connexion of Old and New Testaments must give account of his understanding of the Bible as a whole, that is, above all of the theological problems that arise from the variety of the biblical witness considered in relation to its inner unity.[231]

Ebeling's questions, characterized by his usual clarity and analytical powers, have remained of fundamental importance in discussions of 'biblical theology'. This can easily be seen by examining two publications, both central to the theme, which appeared in 1970. Both Hans-Joachim Kraus[232] and Brevard S. Childs[233] deal with fundamental questions concerning the possibility and the prospects of biblical theology, and both are to a remarkable degree engaged in the same problems that were pointed out by Ebeling.

However, Kraus and Childs not only share many of their basic questions, but even the solutions they suggest seem to converge to a great extent. Some of the similarities may in fact be more apparent than real. Evidently, the two authors have very different backgrounds and horizons in so far as Kraus stands firmly within the German theological tradition and mainly relates his discourse to the hermeneutical debate of the 1960s, whilst Childs is theologically at home in an Anglo-American context. Even the ways in which Kraus and Childs use the term 'biblical theology' differ. For Kraus 'biblical theology' designates a theological discipline which is, for all practical purposes, more a *desideratum* than a reality. Childs, on the other hand, comes from the background of the 'Biblical Theology Movement', and is able to use the expression 'biblical theology' to denote endeavours and tendencies which are already historical phenomena. Nevertheless, it is doubtlessly justified to regard the books by Kraus and Childs as signs of a major trend in post-war theology.

Common to Kraus and Childs is the feeling of being in a stage of transition, which necessitates a careful statement of affairs in order that progress can be made. Accordingly, both devote considerable space to historical retrospects. Furthermore, Kraus and Childs share the conviction that 'biblical theology' is the key word for a task of decisive importance to present-day theology. There may be a characteristic difference between European and American theology involved when Kraus is primarily concerned with the situation of theological scholarship,[234] whereas Childs has in view, above all, the 'practical needs' for a new biblical theology. The danger of fragmentation which threatens biblical scholarship, increased through the massive expansion of archaeological and historical knowledge (Ugarit, Qumran, Nag Hamadi, etc.), the impact of political and social change and the challenge it represents to the Church, and the practical need of Christian pastors, all render a proper biblical theology urgently necessary, according to Childs.[235]

Both Kraus and Childs focus on the canonical status of the Bible as something of fundamental importance to biblical theology. The biblical texts in their present shape and context, Kraus argues, remain the basis for biblical theology. A 'historical truth' behind or outside the biblical documents can be of no primary interest to biblical theology.[236] And Kraus also attempts to make 'canon' the point of departure for biblical hermeneutics. For exegetes, the canon is a guide to a context within which they can expect to experience and understand the authentic testimony to the Word of God.[237] In this interpretation of 'canon' Kraus clearly reveals himself as a disciple of Karl Barth. Likewise, Childs regards the canon as the proper context for doing biblical theology, and as a hermeneutical principle.[238] When it comes to the implications of this principle for practical biblical exegesis, both Kraus and Childs denounce procedures that isolate the texts, and plead for an 'openness' towards the 'canonical' context.[239] In particular, Kraus points to the possibility of investigating themes common to Old and New Testaments as a desirable project for a biblical theology.[240] Childs suggests starting from the specific OT passages quoted in the NT, and thence proceeding to more general thematic analyses.[241]

Two major problems, both already emphasized by Ebeling, would seem to lie at the heart of recent endeavours in the field of biblical theology. The first problem may for the sake of convenience be termed that of scriptural unity, and the second that of scriptural relevance.

The variety of diverging religious and theological ideas and perspectives found in the various biblical books and in the different strata within individual books or even individual texts, may indeed make it difficult to recognize any continuity or any common message in the Bible. 'Biblical theology', it would seem, is often conceived of as the projected explication of the 'inner unity' of the biblical writings. However, the question is what sort of unity is intended, or on which level this unity is sought. A glance at the tradition of Protestant theology may serve to illustrate the question. Traditionally, the assumption that the Bible has its unity in the gospel of Christ is regarded as the axiom which renders theology possible. And this theological 'centre' of Scripture cannot be assessed without considering its present-day significance. In this perspective, the very nature of the unity of Scripture, a unity which cannot be separated from theological interpretation, would not seem to recommend the creation of a special discipline to explain it. Rather, it would appear to be the proper task of systematic theology to give account of the unity of Scripture, not in the form of exegesis or historical description, but in the form of valid theological statements with regard to today's situation.

The problem of scriptural relevance or of historical and contemporary meanings of Scripture is caused by the undeniable distance between the historical world in which the books of the Bible are at home, and out of which they speak, and the world of contemporary man. Evidently, the problem of scriptural relevance in this sense may be regarded as a special case of the general 'hermeneutical' problem, although admittedly a particularly important case, since it involves questions fundamental to the identity of the Christian religion. Probably no theologian in the twentieth century has been more directly concerned with the hermeneutical problem than Rudolf Bultmann. His programme may be summarized as taking seriously without restrictions the presuppositions inherent in modern man's perception of reality, whilst at the same time insisting on the existential relevance of the gospel testified to by the NT. Bultmann has, of course, been widely criticized, most notaby by Karl Barth and his followers for undertaking an illegitimate reduction of the biblical contents to anthropological rather than theological categories. The question remains, though, how the universe of the Bible is, or can be, related to contemporary conditions.

Here again 'biblical theology' is often expected to have salutary effects. However, it is necessary to ask whether the problem at stake is really of such nature that a solution can be expected from the development of a special theological discipline. Biblical theology, when advocated as a means of hermeneutical bridge-building, is usually supposed to overcome the gulf between biblical exegesis and systematic theology. Biblical theology, it is hoped, should enable the theologian to make statements which are both valid for our time and organically rooted in the biblical testimony. Now, there is in fact much evidence which suggests that, for all practical purposes, the alleged gulf between exegesis and theology has generally been much less significant than often assumed. Some of the most prominent biblical scholars in modern times have been both strongly influenced by, and have themselves made remarkable impacts on systematic theology. This is certainly true of such giants as Rudolf Bultmann and Gerhard von Rad in the fields of NT and OT studies respectively. And it is evident that the development of OT exegesis in the twentieth century can only be properly understood when seen in connection with the history of systematic theology in the same period. On the other hand, however, the problem of biblical exegesis and systematic theology has deeper reasons than usually recognized. It is hardly too much to say that theology has long been marked by a high degree of embarrassment, whether admitted or not, as far as its relation to the Bible is concerned. The obligation to be in some sense 'biblical' or to have some sort of 'scriptural base' for one's statements is essential to Christian theology, and in particular to theology in the Protestant tradition. Since the Enlightenment the uncertainty as to the practical implications of this obligation has become ever more fundamental despite all tendencies in the opposite direction. The embarrassment may be described as that of having a Bible which is really supposed to be the norm and base for theology and preaching, and yet not knowing how to appropriate the historical contents of this Bible. This is an embarrassment which affects contemporary theology in its entirety, unless it chooses either to be mere reformulation of traditional doctrines, or to dispense altogether with any obligation to Christian tradition.

The quest for a 'biblical theology' and the expectation that it may somehow be able to reconcile biblical exegesis and systematic theology may well be a symptom of this fundamental 'crisis of relevance' in contemporary theology. If this is true, it does not require much proof to show that this theological crisis cannot be solved by establishing new disciplines, but calls, above all, for reflection in the field of systematic theology. At the same time, though, it should be acknowledged that the quest for a biblical theology reflects a widespread recognition of the crisis and a will to overcome it. In this sense, the endeavours to define a biblical theology also bear witness to the fact that theology has not, as a whole, entirely forgotten its 'scriptural' obligation.

PART II
PROSPECTS OF OLD TESTAMENT THEOLOGY

Chapter 3

THEOLOGY AND THE BIBLE

In the preceding chapter we have focused on some of the most important problems which have been discussed in relation to OT theology. My aim is now to offer some constructive suggestions as to the prospects and possibilities of that discipline. Obviously, in some sense or other OT theology must be described as a section of 'biblical' theology. Therefore, it will be necessary to introduce some further observations on the nature of biblical theology, in order to assess how the purpose and procedure of OT theology should be understood within this wider context.

The theme of 'biblical theology' naturally leads to a consideration of the fundamental relationship between theology and the Bible. The role of the Bible in Christian theology may, of course, be described in terms of a historical investigation of how the Bible has actually functioned throughout Church history. On the other hand, the significance of the Bible may also be defined theologically in normative statements, which intend to determine how the Bible ought to function. The historical and the theological aspects should not be confused, but neither can they be entirely separated.

1. *The Bible as Canon*

A long theological tradition, including Patristic theology, medieval scholasticism, and the theological mainstream of Reformation and Protestant Orthodoxy, defines the role and significance of the Bible by pointing to the biblical books as the authentic documents of divine revelation. The Bible, according to this tradition, has a normative and authoritative function within Christian theology, for in the Bible the Church has to do with the revelation that constitutes her existence. Naturally the biblical revelation is not necessarily regarded as the only possible source of theological knowledge. Theology may well be able to draw valid conclusions from the facts of nature or from other areas of human experience. In fact, in most periods of the past there has been a legitimate 'natural theology' owing its knowledge to what has often been called God's 'natural revelation' in the created world. However, the specifically Christian insights have always been regarded as derived from the 'supernatural' revelation evidenced in the Bible. Certainly, the methods and principles according to which the biblical documents have been employed in the construction of theological doctrines have varied enormously in the history of Christian theology. Still, the normative function ascribed to the Bible as the authentic witness to divine revelation is an integral element in Christian tradition. Although this is in principle a historically descriptive statement, it follows that Christian theology must in some way affirm the authority of the Bible if it is not to lose its historical identity.

Theology, then, has to do with the Bible in its normative function. The same thing may be expressed by saying that theology has to do with the Bible in its function as canon. Such a usage of the word 'canon' is current in modern theological literature. It may well be, of course, that the term originally had a rather more narrow or formal significance, and that it primarily meant the exactly defined body of writings recognized as Holy Scripture.[1] There would, however, be little point in arguing for a restrictive usage of the word 'canon' in this formal sense. In the theological debate of the twentieth century 'canon' has come to mean the Bible in its function as the basis for the preaching and teaching of the Church. Possibly, this terminology may be criticized as imprecise, but the fact remains that it has become established.

It is of great importance that the Church acknowledges the Bible as canon in this sense. The primary function of the canon is to serve as a criterion for the authenticity of Christian theology and preaching. This in itself implies that there exists something which deserves the name 'authentic Christianity'. Not every statement made in a theological or ecclesiastical context can rightly claim to be authentically Christian, and the criterion for assessing its authenticity must somehow be sought in its relation to Holy Scripture. Then, there is a further important implication of the canonical status of the Bible. 'Authentic Christianity' is in a sense something historical. There is an 'original revelation' to which the Church remains bound, in the sense that what the Church preaches and teaches must in some way or other be related to her origins. This gives the canonical Scripture a critical or 'anti-authoritarian' function over against later traditions of the Church. In itself Scripture belongs to the tradition of the Christian community. Nevertheless, in its canonical function the Bible is distinguished from all other traditions as a critical norm.

This separation of Scripture from tradition has often been judged arbitrary, partly because it has in the past frequently been linked to untenable positions regarding the 'supernatural' origin of the Bible. It is evident that the exact limits of the canon cannot be vindicated on theological grounds, since the inclusion or exclusion of particular books has frequently been an open question in Christian tradition. But the importance of distinguishing Scripture from tradition lies elsewhere. It has to do, in fact, with the fundamental structure of the Christian religion. We observed above that the teaching and preaching of the Church must be related to her origins. This relationship, however, is neither automatic nor simply established through the tradition of the Church. Ecclesiastical authority, or, for that matter, any other present authority, cannot guarantee that what the Church preaches and teaches is in fact authentic Christianity. In a certain sense each generation has to return to the origins in the same quest for authenticity. Certainly, theological tradition may provide guidance of inestimable importance for interpreting and understanding the Christian message. But authentic Christianity is in principle not something which can simply be taken over from tradition. This critical or anti-authoritarian function is what is theologically implied in the distinction between Scripture and tradition.

So far I have attempted to describe the canonical function of the Bible in very formal terms. What, then, is this Holy Scripture which is supposed to function as a normative criterion and a critical norm for the preaching and teaching of the Christian Church? From a historical point of view, the answer must be that Holy Scripture is primarily the books of the OT. This may at first glance seem a surprising statement. However, it is a historical fact that the OT was the Bible of the primitive Church, probably with the inclusion of a more or less specified number of writings which later came to be categorized as Apocrypha or Pseudepigrapha. Thus, whilst there was at one time a Christian Church that did not know a NT canon, the

Church was never without the Scripture of the OT, although it may well have ascribed little importance to the exact definition of a body of holy writings.

It is interesting to notice that this historical priority of the OT as Holy Scripture over against the NT was clearly recognized by some of the Reformers, notably by Martin Luther. According to Luther, 'Scripture' in the proper sense means the OT. The gospel of the 'NT', properly speaking, is not essentially 'Scripture', but oral proclamation, although at a certain stage the preaching of Christ and the Apostles was fixed in literary form. Moreover, this preaching was related to the OT Scriptures in the sense that Christ and the Apostles provided a new and appropriate interpretation of these writings as prophecy. In other words, the NT is the key to understanding the OT, which alone deserves the name 'Scripture' in its original and proper meaning.[2] Luther's position, although it presupposes the 'pre-critical' view of the OT as containing direct and literal predictions of Jesus Christ and his ministry, includes a remarkably precise understanding of the historical meaning of 'Holy Scripture' in the NT context.

The priority of the OT as Holy Scripture in early Christianity is a historical fact. This implies that the authority of the OT for the Christian Church is in a certain sense given *a priori*. From the moment when the Church came into being the OT was 'there' as Holy Scripture.[3] Far from being a secondary or inferior part of the Bible, requiring a particular defence or justification, the OT is from a historical point of view the Holy Scripture of the Church in the original and proper sense. Clearly, this runs counter to the widespread opinion that Holy Scripture is first and foremost the NT, compared to which the OT has only a secondary value. Naturally, from the historical fact that the OT was from the beginning the Holy Scripture of the Christian Church, we should not automatically make the theological judgment that this ought to be so. Indeed it might be alleged that the Church made a theological mistake in acknowledging the OT as Holy Scripture. This would mean that the way 'Holy Scripture' was understood in the primitive Church and by the NT writers would have to be rejected. If one takes this position, however, it seems rather arbitrary to declare the NT authoritative for the Christian Church as the real 'Holy Scripture'.

If, on the other hand, we accept the traditional position that the Holy Scripture of the Church is primarily the OT, some important theological consequences follow. First, the obvious state of flux of the Old Testament canon in early Christian times should warn us against ascribing too much significance to the exact limitation of the canon. In fact, there has always been considerable variability as to the number of books included in the canon, and this should not be regarded as a serious theological problem. Secondly, insisting on the OT as the primary part of Holy Scripture necessarily implies that scriptural authority has to be defined in a rather flexible and sophisticated manner. A legalistic 'Biblicism' is thus automatically excluded. There can be no question of declaring all statements found in the canonical books immediately and indiscriminately valid and authoritative in relation to present-day Christian preaching and practice. Naturally, such a position would be untenable even if the NT writings alone were to be regarded as canonical. The OT, however, with its variety of themes and literary genres, and its multiplicity of religious and theological ideas and tendencies, makes the absurdity of legalistic 'Biblicism' even more obvious. The normative and critical function of the canon cannot be argued in any simplistic manner. In other words, the problems of interpretation and application have to be addressed when we assert the canonical function of Scripture. How is the Bible to be interpreted, and how are the contents of the biblical books to be applied to the present-day situation, in order that the Bible may exercise its canonical function as norm and criterion?

2. *Principles of Biblical Interpretation*

So far I have attempted to offer some elementary suggestions as to the role and significance of the Bible when seen in a theological perspective. I argued that theology has to do with the Bible as the canon of the Christian Church, and described the canonical function of the Bible as a normative and critical function over against subsequent traditions and developments within Christianity.

What are the implications regarding the principles for interpreting the Bible and, in particular, the OT? The most important implication is that the OT must be read in a historical perspective. In affirming the necessity of historical exegesis there is both a general hermeneutical point and a specifically theological one, and the two are intimately related. Reading a text historically means being concerned with the contents of the text itself, and attempting to understand the text against the situation in which it was written, in so far as this situation can be historically reconstructed. A text is a historical fact. As a text it is only comprehensible within a historical context. The symbols of written language only function semantically when they are related to a system which is historically given. The only alternative to historical reading is to read into the semantic symbols of the text a meaning different from their own. I am fully aware that this is to touch upon complex hermeneutical questions which lie outside the scope of my purposes here. However, it seems evident that the notion of a 'proper meaning' of the text—whether this meaning is to be defined more precisely as the meaning intended by the author or, rather, as the content of the text itself, which can only be fully assessed when the history of the text is taken into consideration—is indispensable if the distinction between understanding a text and not understanding it is to be maintained, that is, if exegesis is to be defended as a meaningful undertaking. The emphasis on the 'proper meaning' also has a strictly theological aspect, directly related to the canonical function of Scripture. Certainly, a historical reading of the biblical texts is required if these texts are to play a normative and critical role over against theological and ecclesiastical tradition. There can obviously be no question of the texts exercising such a critical function if their interpretation is entirely controlled by tradition or, for that matter, by some present-day religious or non-religious ideology. The historical reading, which strives to uncover the 'proper meaning' of the texts, is the only way in which these texts are, at least in principle, taken seriously for what they are.

A classical illustration of this point is found in the exclusive emphasis of the Reformers on the 'literal sense' of the biblical text against allegorical interpretation. Historical-critical exegesis may confidently claim to be in continuity with the Reformation in this respect. Being 'critical' here simply means to ask the questions which the text itself occasions, and consequently to observe the discrepancies and unevenness which the texts may possibly exhibit. Being 'critical' thus means to take the text seriously as it stands; it is exactly the uncritical reading which fails to do this.[4]

In other words, the canonical status of the OT requires a historical-critical reading of it. This implies that the OT should be read for what it is—the national literature of an ancient Near Eastern people. It is a fundamental error, too frequently committed, to isolate the OT from the world of ancient Near Eastern culture and religion, when, in fact, the former is historically a part of the latter. It is wholly legitimate to inquire after the peculiarities and chracteristics of the OT literature over against its general background. Similarly, it is perfectly meaningful to contrast, say, the plays of Shakespeare and the wider world of 'Elizabethan drama'. The mistake occurs when attempts are made at sustaining or supporting the theological relevance of the OT by isolating it from its historical and cultural environment. In the American Biblical Theology Movement this was a very marked tendency. Similar inclinations, though, can very easily be found in continental OT theology.

Hans Walter Wolff, in a long essay on OT hermeneutics in 1956, devoted a special section to demonstrating that the OT literature cannot possibly be understood 'in terms of its environment'.[5] His argumentation partly rests on a rather superficial depreciation of ancient Near Eastern religion,[6] but mainly he is concerned to show how the genuinely Israelite conception of God, of divine law, and of state and kingship, is entirely different from what Israel's neighbours thought about these things.[7] It is certainly true that the religion of the OT includes features unparalleled by other religious documents from the ancient Near East. There would seem, however, to be little historical basis for insisting on some absolute contrast between the OT and ancient Near Eastern culture, or for declaring the OT 'a stranger' within its environment.[8] In the years since Wolff's essay there has been a growing acknowledgment amongst scholars that Israel's culture and religion in the pre-exilic period were much more akin to the religious and cultural thought-world of its ancient Near Eastern environment. However, the idea of a fundamental contrast remains influential, but is often based upon a simplistic theological evaluation: whatever is 'genuinely Israelite' is often more or less expressly identified with divine revelation,[9] whilst religious ideas that were 'taken over' by the Israelites from other ancient Near Eastern religions are assumed to be extraneous to revelation. In other words, to show that an idea found in the OT was 'taken over' from Israel's 'environment' is to deprive that idea of its revelatory character. Usually, this identification of the 'genuinely Israelite' with divine revelation is undertaken without due reflection. However, it is neither historically nor theologically valid. Historically, the OT must be interpreted within the context of the ancient Near Eastern culture to which it belongs. The contrasts, which are certainly not to be overlooked, can from a historical point of view only be of a relative nature.

Theologically, the relevance and authority of the OT cannot be supported by isolating it from the historical context in which it is at home. Rather, the relevance and authority of the OT are implied in its canonical status.

In the canonical status of the OT within the Christian Church lies the presupposition that the OT texts, when read historically and critically, that is with due respect for their actual contents, can and should be a critical norm for preaching the gospel of Christ. In view of this, the programme of 'Christological' OT interpretation, advocated most notably by Wilhelm Vischer[10] is fundamentally mistaken. The programme is best understood as dictated by fear or doubt that the OT does not, in fact, possess that relevance for Christian theology and preaching which is implied in its canonical status. What the 'Christological' interpretation tries to do, then, is to secure this relevance by reading something into the OT texts which they do not really contain. But the normative and critical relevance of the OT cannot be saved through an exegesis of this sort, which arguably comes close to intellectual dishonesty. Either the OT is relevant when interpreted loyally—and this necessarily means historically and critically—or it is not relevant at all.

To say that the relevance of the OT is presupposed in its canonical status is not the same thing as to show and explain wherein this relevance lies. As we have seen, however, the canonical status of the OT within the Christian Church is a historical fact. Of course, when the early Christians regarded the sacred books of Judaism as their Holy Scripture, this had to do with the religion-historical situation in which the Christian religion originated. The Jewish religion provided the framework within which both Jesus and his first believers understood themselves and their faith. In this sense, the identity between Yahweh Lord of Hosts the God of Israel and God the Father of Jesus Christ is a religion-historical fact. In other words, there is an indisputable historical continuity between the religion of the OT and the Christian religion, a continuity which, of course, also comprises the development of Judaism in the period between OT and NT times.

It is clear, however, that there is historical discontinuity as well. Both from a religion-historical point of view and in its self-understanding the Christian religion became something new and different from Judaism, although the time of the transformation is admittedly very difficult to identify with any historical precision.

The continuity, though, is clearly the inner reason for the canonical status of the OT within a Christian context.

It goes without saying that no theological conclusions can be automatically derived from the religion-historical continuity between the OT and Christianity. However, in acknowledging the OT as its canonical Scripture the Christian Church affirms the theological validity of this continuity. It lies in the nature of this position that, ultimately, it must remain open to conjecture. On the one hand, the Bible is given *a priori* as Holy Scripture within the Church, and its canonical status cannot be demonstrated *a posteriori* by historical or theological arguments. On the other hand, the only way in which the normative and critical function of Scripture implied in its canonical status can be applied is through an appeal to the contents of the biblical texts themselves.

Theologically, it is necessary to affirm that there is indeed a 'centre' in the OT, and, furthermore, that this 'centre' is in a certain sense the Christian gospel. Speaking in traditional terms, we may say that Jesus Christ is the 'scope' of the entire Holy Scripture.[11] Clearly, this is a theological statement which cannot be vindicated by means of exegetical analysis. Still, in this theological statement is contained an exhortation to consider the evidence and judge whether or not such a statement makes sense. Although, strictly speaking, the statement that Jesus Christ is the scope of Scripture cannot be validated exegetically, it still claims to be meaningful when viewed against the biblical material. This implies that the continuity between the OT and Christianity is in some sense organically related to the ministry of Christ.[12]

Only careful exegetical study of the OT texts can show whether the notion of such an organic continuity with Christ as the centre can be said to make sense. It is possible in very general terms to point to some obvious ways in which the contents of the OT relate organically to the Christian gospel. In the OT prophets a religious universalism is conceived, which may or may not have close parallels and antecedents in previous Israelite and Near Eastern religion. At any rate, the universalist conception of Yahweh as the supreme ruler of the world, and the ethical responsibility of all nations before him, is presented by the prophets with unprecedented consistency and clarity. The lines which connect this prophetic universalism with the proclamation of Christ as saviour of the world are easily demonstrable. Then again, the Deuteronomistic history offers an interpretation of the entire history of the Israelite people, a history which is presented both as a salvation history and as a history of judgment. The grace of Yahweh and the disobedience of the people are the two decisive factors in the Deuteronomistic conception. It does not require much proof to show that the same motifs are central in the NT interpretation of the ministry and death of Jesus Christ. Through historical observations of this type, biblical theology cannot demonstrate or justify the authority and relevance of the OT for the Christian religion, but it can certainly show that the appeal to the OT as canon is actually far from being meaningless.

With these remarks we have already anticipated the following description of the discipline biblical theology; and we must now, having to some extent clarified the theological position from which the whole enterprise of biblical studies is here viewed, proceed to sketch how that discipline, and, in particular, the discipline of Old Testament theology, may be defined within this perspective.

Chapter 4

BIBLICAL THEOLOGY—SOME PROPOSITIONS

In the preceding chapter we were led, through reflecting upon the
canonical function of the Bible, to acknowledge the theological
necessity of studying the Bible historically and critically. The
purpose of this chapter is to describe more precisely how biblical
theology can be conceived of as a historical discipline, and, more
specifically, to sketch a model for an Old Testament theology. This
model, it should be emphasized, does not pretend to be anything
more than a rough sketch, merely intended to indicate in what
direction an Old Testament theology, written according to the
principles advocated here, could be pursued, and to point out some of
the problems which this discipline has to address.

1. *The Task of Biblical Theology*

In a certain sense, there would seem to be good reasons for following
the tradition of Protestant Orthodoxy in defining biblical theology as
a subsidiary discipline which is necessary for practical purposes. It
may be suggested, however, that this discipline should be regarded as
an adjunct to biblical exegesis rather than dogmatics; and in this
respect we are in agreement with the theological tradition that has
developed since the Enlightenment. The task of biblical theology
may then be described as the completing and summarizing of
exegetical results. Whilst biblical exegesis is concerned with analysing
individual texts or books of the Bible, biblical theology attempts to
establish the main lines within each book, and to explain how the
concepts and ideas of the various parts of the Bible are interrelated.[1]
Biblical theology, in other words, is a historical and descriptive
discipline rather than a normative and prescriptive one. It belongs to
the realm of historical theology, not to that of systematic theology. In

practice, biblical theology may well be able to play an important part as something like a bridge between exegesis and systematic theology, in so far as it provides the systematic theologian with a very useful summary of the ways in which current biblical scholarship reads the Bible and of the main results reached by the exegetes. Such a bridge-building task, however, is not, properly speaking, to be included in the definition of biblical theology. Biblical theology is not to be regarded as some sort of addition to historical biblical studies, but as the indispensable, concluding part of biblical exegesis, the part concerned with the more wide-ranging perspectives. Major themes connecting various parts of the biblical literature are the proper subject matter of biblical theology. Now, such themes may well turn out to be of the greatest interest for systematic theology. But biblical theology does not automatically provide us with any information as to whether the themes to which it points in a certain case are important in the present-day situation; and the possible theological 'usefulness' of its results should not, as a rule, be allowed to determine the perspective of biblical theology.

Thus, biblical theology carries out historical investigations of major themes and problems within biblical literature. This implies that no sharp distinction is possible between this type of investigation, belonging to biblical theology, and some of the more wide-ranging exegetical and religion-historical studies, which are conventionally not thus designated. Nor, indeed, is there any reason why such an unambiguous distinction should be desired. The characteristic feature of biblical theology is its interest in major religious motifs and decisive lines of religious development in so far as they are reflected in the biblical texts. In particular, biblical theology is concerned with the historical influence exercised by certain ideas or texts in subsequent tradition. Biblical theology in this sense is a field in which much fruitful work has been done, although very often the specific term 'biblical theology' may not have been used. An obvious example of a work which fully deserves to be counted as biblical theology is the inquiry into OT covenant theology by Lothar Perlitt, which appeared in 1969.[2] Here, problems are addressed which in many respects determine the perspective in which large parts of the biblical literature are read and interpreted. At the same time Perlitt's book is a religion-historical study, providing an excellent illustration of the significance of historical reconstructions for our interpretation of the Bible.

However, for more specific didactic purposes, a comprehensive course-book on biblical theology is also required. The purpose of such books is to provide theological students and scholars of other disciplines with a general survey of the state of this discipline at a certain point of time. For this purpose, the conventional division of biblical theology into the sections 'OT theology' and 'NT theology' is very practical. What occasions this division is the recognition of the historical and literary differences between the writings of the OT and the NT, and, in principle, it has nothing to do with the theological 'unity of Scripture'. As stated above, such a 'unity' is to be sought at a different level, and is a matter for systematic theology to consider. How to organize the historical discipline of biblical theology is merely a question of how to meet the practical demands of the material. The structure of an 'OT theology' within this framework will be our theme in the following concluding section.

2. *Old Testament Theology—Structure and Procedure*

The purpose of an 'Old Testament theology' is to present a summarizing description of the most important motifs, themes, and problems within the literature of the OT. In accordance with the principles set out above, this is a historical undertaking, which presupposes both the detailed exegesis of the various OT texts and books, and the broader investigations of religion-historical main themes and developments within larger sections of the OT. As pointed out in Part I, the most appropriate organization of an OT theology has been a much debated issue, the main alternatives being a 'historical' or diachronic arrangement and a 'systematic', or synchronic one. Since OT theology is here viewed as a 'historical' discipline in the fundamental sense, we have to do with a choice only between different modes of structuring the historical survey, and not between entirely different viewpoints. The decision must depend on what suits the subject matter of an OT theology best.

The diversity of religious and theological ideas within the various parts of the OT was a recurrent theme in our survey of the scholarly debate in Part I. As observed by von Rad[3] and many others, the books of the OT do not contain 'a theology', but a variety of different 'theologies'. This fact is a strong argument for choosing a 'historical', or diachronic, structure, rather than a 'systematic', or synchronic, cross-section. In other words, an OT theology should not be structured in accordance with theological categories or concepts more or less like those found in a traditional course-book on dogmatics, but should follow a historically oriented scheme. The question is, then, what sort of historical scheme is to be adopted. Usually, 'historically' oriented OT theologies have been organized in accordance with the chronological development of Israelite religion, as the various authors would reconstruct it. However, OT theology does not primarily deal with the religion of Israel, but with the literature of the OT. Consequently, the most appropriate guideline for the structure of OT theology is provided by the main literary genres of the OT. Broadly speaking, this was the principle which governed the OT theology of von Rad.[4] As he observed, such a structure implies that there is a high degree of affinity between OT theology and OT introduction. On the other hand, there are considerable differences as well. OT introduction focuses on questions of date, authorship, etc., concerning the books and texts of the OT. Questions of this type are for the most part not essential to OT theology. Here the subject matter is the contents of the OT writings, and it may, at least in a number of instances, be perfectly possible to analyse these contents in an appropriate manner even when no conclusive answers have been given to the introductory questions.[5]

Properly speaking, the literary genres of the OT are very numerous. Some genres may be reasonably clearly defined, whilst others would seem to overlap in a way that renders any attempt at a precise definition a hazardous enterprise. Ever since the introduction of modern form-critical research OT scholars have devoted considerable interest to the problem of assigning the OT texts to their proper genres. The debates and discussions clearly demonstrate that many OT texts cannot be unambiguously classified as belonging to one genre or another, and in a number of cases the texts, as we have them, are the result of a combination of several genres. Consequently, it would scarcely be possible, or, indeed, practical for an OT theology to attempt to assign every individual text to a fully appropriate literary genre. Accordingly, it is best simply to divide the literature of the OT into a few main, and commonly accepted categories. The scheme at which I arrive is as follows.

A.   Wisdom
B.   Psalmic literature
C.   Narrative literature

D.   Law
E.   Prophecy

The order in which these categories have been placed requires some explanatory comments. It will be clear at a glance that they are not set out in a chronological order. Rather, the arrangement suggested here reflects certain basic viewpoints as to what is primary and secondary in Israelite religion, as it is exhibited in the OT.

The order proposed above differs entirely from the way in which the literary materials of the OT were arranged by von Rad in his OT theology. The differences have to do with the development of OT scholarship since the appearance of von Rad's work. Thus, it is significant that the first volume of his OT theology deals with the 'historical traditions' and the second volume with the 'prophetic traditions' of Israel. This structure obviously has to do with von Rad's conviction that Israelite religion was from its earliest origins distinguished by historical interest, and expressed itself accordingly in the form of historical narrative. For this reason, von Rad begins by focusing on the narrative literature, which in a sense provides the basis for the rest of his work, whilst Psalms and wisdom literature are treated more like a commentary or a supplement to the core of narrative material. The prophets of the Old Testament are then interpreted against this background, and represented as critical revisers of the traditions extant in the historical literature. The emphasis on the narrative parts of the Old Testament is retained, yet at the same time prophecy is acknowledged to be a factor of decisive, independent importance. It could be argued that the structure underlying von Rad's OT theology represents a synthesis of two different historical perspectives. His work may be said to follow the course of both the history of Israelite religion and the history of OT literature. From the point of view of literary history, the composition of his two volumes reflects the idea that Israel's historical traditions existed in a fixed form before the emergence of the prophetic literature. And in a religion-historical perspective, von Rad's work reflects the notion that Israelite religion was originally and essentially a historically oriented religion, which only at a later stage became 'eschatological', as the preaching of the prophets reveals.

To claim that von Rad's view of Israelite religion and the development of OT literature has been proven wrong, would be a gross simplification. However, in OT scholarship since von Rad there has been a marked tendency to shift the emphasis. Notably, greater significance has been ascribed to wisdom literature within the whole of the OT. Moreover, the primary importance of historical narrative as a characteristic of Israelite religion has been questioned in various ways by scholars such as James Barr[6] and Bertil Albrektson.[7] Then again, an alternative to von Rad's conception of Israelite religion is the reconstruction advocated by Hans Heinrich Schmid in a number of works.[8] Schmid sees the religion of Israel as essentially a variant of ancient Near Eastern religion, a variant which, however, in the course of time, undergoes a peculiar development. During most of the pre-exilic period, according to Schmid, the mainstream of Israelite religion, both in its 'official' and its 'popular' aspects, differed little from the religious convictions and practices of the neighbouring peoples. Above all, pre-exilic Yahwism was concerned with cosmic and social order and stability rather than with history. It was the influence of the great prophets and the impact of the national catastrophe which befell Israel in the eighth to sixth centuries that led to her radical departure from the common basic scheme of Near Eastern religion. Although many scholars remain sceptical about such a radical viewpoint as Schmid's, the shifts in OT research mentioned above are reflected in some more recent OT theologies since von Rad, for example Zimmerli's,[9] and especially Westermann's.[10]

These shifts within OT scholarship provide the general background for the model suggested above. The more detailed reasons for setting out the categories in the proposed order will appear from the following remarks, which will deal with each of these categories in turn.

A. *Wisdom*
In OT scholarship the term 'wisdom' is used in several ways. First, 'wisdom' means a certain, more or less unambiguously definable body of texts. Secondly, and more broadly, it means something like a stream of tradition which includes certain characteristic patterns and motifs, and, thirdly, it is used to denote a particular way of thinking. It would be difficult to deny that this multiplicity of meanings attached to the term 'wisdom' has occasionally been the cause of some confusion within scholarly discussions.[11] It goes without saying that there are close relations between the three aspects of 'wisdom' just mentioned. Wisdom as a stream of tradition reflects a certain way of thinking, and this stream of tradition is most clearly and

characteristically exhibited in the wisdom literature. At any rate, the basis for this initial section of an OT theology remains the texts properly belonging to the category of wisdom literature, i.e. first and foremost Proverbs, Job, and Ecclesiastes, although OT theology, when analysing these writings, necessarily has to concern itself with 'wisdom' in the two wider senses.

It is a primary characteristic of wisdom literature that it formulates statements of timeless and universal validity, and it is no wonder that the anonymous collections of wisdom texts, not to mention the individual proverbs and rules, are often difficult to date with any probablity. We have little reason to doubt, though, that the roots of the OT wisdom literature are to be sought in an early stage of Israelite history. Indeed, from the combined evidence of ancient Near Eastern parallels and the explicit witness of the OT, we may safely infer that there was an institutional 'wisdom' in Israel from early monarchical time onwards.

As a way of thinking, wisdom is rooted in the immediate experience of daily life. In wisdom—in Israel as in the whole of the ancient Near East—people are engaged in a continuous struggle to understand, to interpret, and to relate actively to reality, as they encounter it in its variety of phenomena and situations. The results of these endeavours are seen in the rules and sentences of wisdom literature. At a more advanced level, however, wisdom involves the conception of a comprehensive world-view, in which cosmological and ethical laws and regularities are ascertained. It would seem in many respects justified to argue that this understanding of reality, which may be called the theme of OT wisdom literature, forms an important part of the background for most of the literature in the OT. Thus, H.H. Schmid has convincingly shown that even large parts of the historical and narrative literature in the OT are structured according to motifs known from wisdom literature.[12] The Deuteronomists depict Israelite history as a sequence of sins against Yahweh, sins which are then inevitably punished, and meritorious deeds, which are always appropriately rewarded, thus clearly reflecting the scheme of just retribution familiar to us from wisdom literature. Likewise, the presence of motifs known from wisdom literature in the prophetic writings and in the legal literature of the OT has been pointed out by many scholars. All this may serve to illustrate how wisdom, understood as a pattern of thought, is a very broad phenomenon, the basic characteristics of which are reflected with particular clarity in the books we term 'wisdom literature', although the same ideas would seem to have left their mark on considerable portions of the OT.

This section of an OT theology should attempt, then, to establish the main lines of thought and the most important motifs at home in OT wisdom literature. The religious implications of this literature have been evaluated very differently by various scholars. In an early essay on the 'structure' of OT wisdom,[13] Walther Zimmerli states that wisdom literature finds its point of orientation in the question of what is good for the individual. OT wisdom, according to Zimmerli, regards the individual as, ideally speaking, autonomous and independent, and surveys the world around in search for opportunities and options, but with no regard to absolute duties. The ultimate purpose of wisdom is safety, and death, accordingly, is the ultimate evil, something to be avoided at all costs. When wisdom speaks of a divine order, what is meant is in reality an order that is able to guarantee the life and happiness of the individual. On the other hand, von Rad has presented quite a different interpretation.[14] Israelite wisdom literature, he argues, is to be understood in the wider context of Israelite religion. In itself wisdom has no competence in cultic or religious affairs, and it is precisely because of their reverence for Israel's Yahwist faith that the wisdom writers make no attempts at interfering in such matters beyond their range. The proper field of Israelite wisdom is the vast area of human life which is not directly governed by divine commandments or by traditional, well-established legal practice. Here wisdom offers rational advice to guide the young and unexperienced, and to facilitate the decisions of the individual, and, consequently, it assumes the form of flexible, realistic instruction. In Israel, von Rad proceeds, it was a matter of course that Yahweh was the ultimate cause behind the order and regularity found in the world. However, if wisdom literature does not seem to have much to say of Yahweh in explicit terms, it is not due to any sceptical or irreligious attitude, but to an awareness that the majesty of Yahweh is far beyond the limited competence of wisdom.

Undoubtedly OT wisdom literature, as we have it, is the result of a long history, and perspectives and viewpoints may have undergone many changes in the course of time. The obvious point of departure for describing the essential intentions of OT wisdom literature will be found in the book of Proverbs. Here the basic themes are most clearly and unambiguously expressed. The possibilities and consequences of human behaviour are considered in many sayings, and retribution and divine justice are recurrent themes. It certainly seems possible to speak, as does H.H. Schmid, of 'world order' as a prominent theme in these texts, which consistently urge the belief in an orderly universe, governed by just and irresistible laws. As for the further religious implications discussed by Zimmerli and von Rad, it should be noted that this type of literature is originally universal and international, and there would appear to be few differences between the fundamental outlook in many of the older texts in Proverbs and the basic ideas of Egyptian and Mesopotamian wisdom literature. This we may claim with a high degree of certainty in view of the fact that Prov. 22.17-24.22 is, in all probability, directly dependent on the Egyptian wisdom text known as the Instruction of Amenemope.[15] A scrutiny of the Egyptian and Hebrew texts reveals that, apart from the adaptations and alterations suggested by local difference which were to be expected, no rigid 'Yahwistic' reworking of the Egyptian original has taken place in Proverbs. It may be that the specific references to a 'professional' elite which can be traced in the Egyptian instruction have to some degree been deliberately removed, thus rendering the teaching of the Hebrew text applicable to a broader public, and in itself, of course, such a process of 'democratization' is far from insignificant. Doubtless, a marked, outspoken Yahwist tendency is also found in some of the texts in Proverbs, but it seems reasonable to ascribe them to a rather late stage in the redactional history of the book.[16] Such tendencies, which strive to integrate the older wisdom texts into a later form of Yahwist religion, should also be noted and described within the framework of an OT theology.

Against this background, then, an OT theology would be able to turn to the books of Job and Ecclesiastes, in which some of the ideas fundamental to the wisdom of Proverbs are radically questioned, and attempt to explain how the resulting crisis is seen in these very different, yet in certain regards parallel writings. Job presents itself as a classical paradigm of the problem posed to the religious world-view of wisdom literature by the fact that a righteous man has to suffer at the hands of God, a problem which seems to have been considered as early as Sumerian times.[17] And Ecclesiastes contains a more intellectually oriented questioning of the validity of traditional viewpoints on the universe as ordered according to just and intelligible principles. The problem is, in short, whether the traditional world-view can be retained when it is confronted with actual human experience.

B. *Psalmic literature*

When we speak of 'psalmic literature' as the second category to be treated in an OT theology, we are fully aware that this is a very imprecise designation. In practical terms, the writings we have in mind are the Psalter, Lamentations and the Song of Songs.

Traditionally, the Psalter has been regarded as a highly significant part of the OT from a theological point of view. In part, this may be due to the fact that many psalms could be read and interpreted in a markedly 'Christian' perspective as more or less testimonies to the ministry of Christ and to the life and experience of the Church and the individual Christian. The advent of historical-critical biblical studies led to a departure from such viewpoints, and the Psalms now came to be regarded as religious poems, in which pious Israelites expressed their faith and their hopes. During this century, however, the perspective in which biblical scholarship has viewed the Psalms of the OT has undergone drastic changes. Of decisive importance were the form-critical viewpoints introduced, above all, by Gunkel, who recognized the connection between certain fixed forms and cultic situations, but nevertheless regarded the Psalms in their present shape as imitations deriving from a later period, where the expressions of individual piety had become independent of their original cultic functions.[18] A further step was taken by Mowinckel, who, strongly influenced by the religion-historical studies of Vilhelm Grønbech and Johannes Pedersen, interpreted a great number of OT psalms as actual cultic poetry, rooted, first and foremost, in the 'Enthronement Festival' of Yahweh, which, according to Mowinckel, was celebrated annually by the Israelites in the autumn season on the occasion of the new year.[19] Although his results have been subject to modification and conjecture, Mowinckel's studies have remained basic to Psalm exegesis. The hypothesis of a pre-exilic 'Enthronement Festival' of such significance as Mowinckel supposed, has been widely challenged. Moreover, the dates of many individual psalms continue to be disputed, and perhaps it is justified to speak of a trend in recent exegesis in favour of a relatively late date for the final redaction of most psalms.[20] Probably, many psalms have in fact been subject to redactional activity reflecting the ideas and hopes of periods subsequent to their original composition. Nevertheless, a number of texts in the Psalter would still seem to have preserved reminiscences of a pre-exilic religion rather different from the 'official' viewpoints of post-exilic Judaism. Polytheistic traits and ideas which apparently reveal a 'Canaanite' background survive in a number of instances, and there are indications that in other cases such traits have been suppressed as a result of redactional activity.

Taking into account the historical development of the literature in question, this section of an OT theology will be able to assert most conveniently the dominant themes and problems in the Psalter by working through the various psalm genres. In the hymns Yahweh is celebrated as creator and ruler of the universe, and sometimes he is depicted as a mythological figure engaged in victorious battle with the powers of chaos, or presiding over a heavenly pantheon of subordinate deities. The royal hymns, in particular, are concerned with the role and function of the Judean king, who is presented as a figure of unique importance within the divinely established order of world and state. In certain passages we are even presented with unambiguous notions of the king as a person of divine qualities. In other words, the maintenance of cosmic and social stability and order would seem to be a theme of major concern to psalms of the types mentioned. And in psalms of lament and thanksgiving the individual, submitting to the will of Yahweh, pleads for justice and happiness, and expresses griefs and trust that Yahweh may grant reintegration into the cosmic and social order. Both hymns and individual laments and prayers have their parallels in religious literature from the Near East outside Israel, and the ideas and motifs they contain would seem to occupy a fundamental position within OT literature comparable to that of the wisdom motifs. The collective, national psalms often recall earlier events of Israelite history, and here motifs peculiar to Israelite religion begin to appear. Finally, in the late didactic poems found in the Psalter all the ideas characteristic of exilic and post-exilic Yahwism are present, such as its occupation with Israel's disobedience towards Yahweh in the past, and the vision of an entirely different future for the nation or its remnants: ideas which have in many cases marked the final redaction of the psalms regardless of their proper literary genre.

Both Lamentations and the Song of Songs will require a particular treatment in an OT theology. Lamentations may be described as an attempt at coping theologically with the national catastrophe of 587

BC. The situation is one of radical crisis for the world-view that had been prevalent in pre-exilic Judah. Both the social and the cosmic order seem to have been disturbed, now Yahweh has cast off his altar, and the anointed of Yahweh, under whose shadow the Judeans had thought to live among the nations, has been taken in the enemies' pits.[21] Finally, in the Song of Songs we encounter an entirely different world and atmosphere, which are, however, also of great significance in what they reveal of the ideas of sexual love in Israel, ideas that may well be implicitly present in a considerable number of places in OT literature.

C. *Narrative literature*
The narrative complexes in the OT, the 'history works' contained in the Pentateuch and the Former Prophets, and in Chronicles, Ezra, and Nehemiah, as well as the minor narrative books of Ruth and Esther, present the interpreter with considerable problems of dating. Moreover, the necessity of distinguishing between the literary works and the traditions behind them adds to the difficulties. Recent tendencies in OT scholarship are in favour of relatively late datings. Much of the literature in question is now ascribed, roughly speaking, to the period around the Babylonian exile. Doubtless, these tendencies represent a justified modification of the chronological picture embraced by the preceding generation of scholars. Still, literature of this sort, as is commonly accepted, seldom emerges out of nothing, and there are, in fact, good reasons to believe that important parts of the traditional material behind the narrative writings have undergone a long and complicated history before the final literary fixation. The picture of Israelite history which the Deuteronomists and the Chroniclers convey was in all probability not the picture of Israelite history extant at the time of Hosea or Amos. Nevertheless, the hints found in the eighth century prophets are sufficiently numerous and unambiguous to demonstrate that traditions concerning Israel's past were certainly known in their days, although we cannot be sure that the contents of such traditions were identical with what we find in the narrative sections of the OT.

The first problem here for an OT theology, the task of which, as we have defined it, is to establish the main lines and themes of the narrative literature, is to determine on which level of this literature the main focus should be concentrated. There are the traditions underlying the texts, traditions which may originally have had a form rather different from their present one, though they are only accessible to us through the transmission provided by the literature. There are the various stages, still in part recognizable, of literary fixation and redaction, on which, however, scholarly opinions differ today as strongly as ever. A glance at the Pentateuch will serve to illustrate what sort of difficulties this situation poses for an OT theology. The traditional picture of the Pentateuch as composed of the four literary documents, or sources, J, E, D, and P, still enjoys the support of the majority of scholars. If these documents are regarded as literary works in the conventional sense, it makes sense to inquire after the religious and other ideas and motifs of each document. Thus Hans Walter Wolff was able, in accordance with this conception, to speak of the *kerygma* of the 'Yahwist'.[22] However, the marked profiles of the traditional documents have been seen to dwindle away in the course of recent research. The existence of a coherent, independent E document has long been disputed, and the studies of Rendtorff and others have challenged the notion of the 'Yahwist' as an independent author to whom a set of definable theological ideas can be ascribed.[23] All in all, then, it would seem to be a highly precarious project to engage in explaining the main ideas of hypothetical works like J or E.

The most advisable procedure for an OT theology, then, will be to deal with the individual tradition complexes found in the Pentateuch and the Book of Joshua, such as the Primeval history, the Patriarchal narratives, the Sojourn in Egypt, the Exodus, the Revelation at Mount Sinai, the Wandering in the Wilderness, and the Settlement in Canaan, and to attempt to draw out their implications, and the motives which may be thought to lie behind their preservation and transmission at various times. It goes without saying that this is necessarily a highly conjectural undertaking, since the reasons that allowed certain traditions to survive and let others fall into oblivion, remain obscure to us in many cases. However, it should be borne in mind that the traditions which did survive constitute not only a religious, but also a national and cultural heritage, and may well have been preserved for exactly this reason. In other words, there is no need to assume that in every single case a 'theological' motive must have dictated the literary fixation or transmission of traditional material. The perspective of an OT theology ought to remain open to alternative possibilities.

The 'history works', or the final redactional complexes of narrative material, also call for analysis and explication within the framework of an OT theology, as far as their major themes and intentions are concerned. Here we would seem to be on much safer ground, since it is the results of this final reworking which are immediately and directly exhibited in the texts, as we now have them. The Deuteronomistic history presents its readers with a distinctive view of Israelite history as governed by human obedience and divine reward on the one hand, and by human disobedience and divine punishment on the other. As remarked above, there would seem to be obvious affinities between this view and some of the ideas basic to OT wisdom literature. Both the Chronicler's version of Israelite history and the final redaction of the Pentateuch are clearly dependent on Deuteronomistic ideas, although both would seem, in more than one respect, to go their own ways.

D. *Law*

In the OT, as it stands, the entire complex of legal literature embedded in the Pentateuch is characterized as divine revelation, ultimately deriving from the utterings of Yahweh at Mount Sinai. The composition of the Pentateuch and the present sequence of Pentateuch and Deuteronomistic history suggest that this revealed 'law' formed the indisputable basis for the following history of the Israelite people, a history which was largely determined by the degree to which the Israelites proved willing to obey the law received through Moses at Mount Sinai. This, of course, became the traditional view of the OT law and its significance. The decisive break was achieved by Julius Wellhausen, who utilized and refined the insights gained through the historical-critical research of numerous scholars before him. For Wellhausen, it was essential that the prophets belonged to an earlier historical stage than the law, and, consequently, that the law should not be made the key to interpreting the prophets.[24] If by 'law' we mean the whole literary complex of laws embodied in the Pentateuch, there can be little doubt that Wellhausen's position was correct. The texts which now form the contents of Yahweh's revelation at Mount Sinai are, in fact, very far from being a homogenous mass. Critical scholars were soon able to identify within this material certain collections, such as the Book of the Covenant, the Holiness Code, the Deuteronomic laws, and the Priestly laws, some of which would appear to have had an independent existence prior to their insertion into the present context. Furthermore the various laws could, on internal grounds, be assigned to different periods in the social and cultural history of ancient Israel. Some of the legal complexes, most notably the Book of the Covenant, might well be of considerable age, but the combination and final redaction of all the texts when they were incorporated into the Sinai narrative, could only be understood as the result of a long development.

This does not mean, however, that Wellhausen's description of the relationship between 'law' and 'prophets' has remained uncontested. In this century, several attempts have been made at showing the dependence of the OT prophets on legal traditions, in particular those legal traditions which were connected with the alleged ancient Israelite amphictyony.[25] Even though these attempts cannot be said, on the whole, to have been sufficiently convincing, the fact remains that the legal literature comprises material which may safely be taken to illustrate Israelite society at a fairly early stage.

The task of an OT theology will be to summarize and present the contents of the various legal collections in the Pentateuch. Theological, ethical, and anthropological motifs should be analysed and explained, and an OT theology ought to consider both how the collections functioned in their original independent form, wherever such a form must be assumed, and the implications of their insertion into the Sinai narrative. Of particular interest are some of the traits that indicate legislative changes with regard to a certain issue. To mention one example, a comparison between the relevant texts in the Book of the Covenant and in Deuteronomy would seem to reveal that at the time of the oldest legal complex a woman was juridically regarded as a piece of property, whereas at a later stage she came to be viewed in some respects as a person.[26] It seems hard to find any other explanation for this than some sort of 'humanistic' influence, however such a notion is to be related to the development of Israelite religion.

The anthologies of Israelite ethics found in the OT in the form of more or less regularly structured series of commandments, prohibitions, curses, or legal principles, deserve special consideration in an OT theology. Albrecht Alt termed these anthologies 'apodictic law', and regarded them as a peculiar Israelite phenomenon, which he then connected with the institutions of 'amphictyony' and 'covenant renewal'.[27] Alt's views have been questioned by many OT scholars, and some have tried to demonstrate that the 'apodictic' genre is in fact paralleled by similar genres in non-Israelite ancient Near Eastern literature. However, no really convincing analogies have so far been shown to match the specific form of a regular series of commandments or prohibitions of this type.[28] On the other hand, the contents of these 'ethical summaries' can hardly be claimed to be as unique or as exclusively Israelite or 'Yahwistic' as Alt would have it, since in many respects they reflect the same sort of ethical principles as the rules and instructions found in wisdom literature in and outside the OT. Still, the anthologies may be significant in a different way. Rather than being the oldest or the most original expressions of Israelite religion, there may be good reasons for seeing in them the result of attempts at summarizing in comprehensive formulations the fundamental demands of Yahwistic ethics. Such attempts would seem to involve a high degree of 'theological' reflection.

E. *Prophecy*

In their present shape, the prophetic books in the OT are collections of disparate materials, and it is obvious that this literature comprises a broad variety of literary genres. Nevertheless, the feature which unites this literature as a particular body within the OT is evident as well. As pointed out by von Rad,[29] it is a striking fact that among the mass of anonymous literature these writings stand out as designated by the names of the individual persons from whom their contents are supposed to derive. This can only be understood as a testimony to the exceptional importance ascribed to these men in the religious and literary history of their people.

However, the precise significance of the prophets in the history of Israelite religion has been subject to very different interpretations. Traditionally, Christian theology has seen the prophets of the OT as preachers of penitence and foretellers of the ministry of Christ. The paradigm for understanding the role of the prophets was, in essentials, provided by the figure of John the Baptist in the NT. As historical-critical research made this notion untenable, theology focused its interest on the religious and ethical teaching of the OT prophets. The generation of OT scholars which largely had its perspective determined by Wellhausen's studies, developed a distinctive and coherent view of OT prophecy. In connection with the reconstruction of Israel's religious history advocated by Wellhausen, the phenomenon of classical prophecy was seen as a decisive factor in the development of Yahwism. The prophets were the representatives of new and more advanced religious and ethical ideas. Accordingly, these scholars were primarily concerned with the prophets as religious personalities, and in their exegesis of the prophetic books they strove, above all, to discover those 'authentic' passages which revealed the personal religious experience of the prophets in question. Broadly speaking, there was a marked change of emphasis in prophetic studies since 1920. Partly, the change must be seen in connection with the new conception of Israel's religious history, based, above all, on the theories of Noth and von Rad, which came to replace the previous reconstruction founded on Wellhausen's ideas. The most important features of Israelite religion were now believed to have existed at a very early historical stage, since the normative traditions found in the OT were mostly dated to a time as early as the pre-monarchical period. The prophets were now largely presented as guardians of these traditions. Form-critical study, which, by definition, focuses on traditional forms and genres, contributed to bringing about an increasing interest in traditional elements in the preaching of the prophets. The institutional side of prophecy was stressed, and, above all, the ties between the prophets and the cult were emphasized in numerous studies. Then again, the growing uncertainty in recent research as to the actual dates of the historical and religious traditions of the OT seems to favour viewpoints that ascribe more importance to the creative endeavours of the OT prophets.

Although much energy has been devoted to attempts at determining the nature of the characteristically 'prophetic' element, that which constitutes a 'prophet', no entirely satisfactory definition has yet been advanced. The fact remains that prophets in Israel must, generally speaking, have been regarded as persons with a definite function in society. The occurrence in the Mari documents of persons acting as spokesmen for the deities[30] suggests a similar function for the prophet in Israel. As far as formal aspects are concerned, no fundamental difference seems to exist between the messengers of ancient Mari and the prophetic figures in Israel known from the OT. On the other hand, few would deny that the prophetic literature of the OT stands out as unique by virtue of the literary qualities and the religious depth that characterize the words of the Israelite prophets. Unlike the divination practice of Mari or, for that matter, of the ancient Near East as a whole, Israelite prophecy came to exercise a decisive influence on the cultural and religious history of the nation within which it occurred.

The most natural starting-point for this final section of an OT theology will be the narrative materials concerned with the early north Israelite prophets found in 1 and 2 Kings. Strictly speaking, these narratives should have been dealt with previously in the section on 'narrative literature', but in practice it would be inappropriate to omit this interesting material from this section. To be sure, the texts in question have been strongly influenced by the views of the Deuteronomistic redaction. However, it is quite possible that they have in a number of instances preserved information about the activities of Israelite prophets at a stage prior to that of classical prophecy. As for the further procedure of an OT theology, a chronological scheme suggests itself as most practical, in so far as the historical order of the prophetic books in the OT can be reconstructed. Thus, following the analyses of the narratives on the early prophetic circles in northern Israel, the literary prophets of the eighth century, the prophets of the exilic era, and the post-exilic prophets should be dealt with in this order. Traditional material used in their preaching must be made subject to tradition-historical analysis. The main emphasis, though, should rest on the intentions and the message of the individual prophets, and on the common features of OT prophecy as a whole. A final section will, of course, have to analyse the visions in the book of Daniel, which take us into the world of Jewish religion at a particular stage, facing the crisis of violent Hellenization during the second century BC.

I have attempted to sketch some of the main problems with which OT theology has to concern itself. It would, no doubt, seem natural for an OT theology written according to the principles sketched above, to be equipped with an introduction informing the reader of the author's viewpoints on the purpose and principles of the discipline 'OT theology' in a wider theological context. From a strictly formal point of view, defining and explaining the theological function and significance of the Bible is a task for dogmatic theology, which, traditionally, includes the *locus* 'De Scriptura Sacra'. For pragmatic reasons, though, it would be appropriate for the author of an OT theology to make his theological presuppositions known to his readers.

If the inclusion of such an introductory section is accepted, although it does not belong to OT theology as such, then the model for a course-book on 'OT theology' would have to look something like the following.

> *Introduction*
> Theology and the Bible—and the
> discipline of biblical theology
>
> A. *Wisdom in the Old Testament*
>   1. Proverbs
>   The main themes of 'wisdom'—'world order'—
>   retribution—divine justice—the theological
>   redaction of Proverbs
>   2. Job
>   The suffering of a righteous man and
>   the problem of divine justice
>   3. Ecclesiastes
>   Questions as to the reality of a just
>   'world order'
>
> B. *Psalmic literature in the Old Testament*
>   1. The Psalter
>   Hymns—individual prayers—collective
>   psalms—didactic poems—other psalms
>   2. Lamentations
>   The crisis of 587 and the attempt at a
>   theological response
>   3. The Song of Songs
>   Sexual love and its interpretation
>
> C. *Narrative literature in the Old Testament*
>   1. The traditions
>   The Primeval history—the Patriarchal
>   narratives—the Sojourn in Egypt—the
>   Exodus—the Revelation at Mount Sinai—
>   the Wandering in the Wilderness—the
>   Settlement in Canaan
>   2. The 'history works'
>   The Deuteronomistic history—the
>   Chronicler—the final redaction of the
>   Pentateuch

D. *Law in the Old Testament*
    1. The major collections
       The Book of the Covenant—the Holiness
       Code—the Deuteronomic laws—the
       Priestly laws
    2. The ethical summaries
    3. The theological redaction of the laws
       in the Pentateuch

E. *Prophecy in the Old Testament*
    1. The narratives on the earliest prophets
    2. The prophetic books in the OT
       The 8th-century prophets—the prophets
       in the era of the Babylonian exile—
       the post-exilic prophets—the book of
       Daniel

Naturally, as a historical discipline OT theology is dependent on the current state of historical and exegetical research. It lies in the nature of historical results that they are constantly open to revision and modification due to the establishing of new facts, the development of new methods, and the elaboration of new theories and insights. Consequently, the task of biblical theology remains a challenge to each generation of biblical scholars, and research in this field is subject to the same process of becoming antiquated which characterizes historical-critical research as a whole. This, in itself, is certainly no reason to lament. On the contrary, it is to be regarded as a welcome sign that the work of the biblical theologian is carried out, as, indeed, is all theological work, under ever-changing conditions. In this lie both its limitations and its freedom.

NOTES

Notes to Chapter 1

1. C. Steuernagel, 'Alttestamentliche Theologie und alttestamentliche Religionsgeschichte', K. Budde, *Vom Alten Testament* (BZAW, 41; 1925), pp. 266-73.

2. O. Eissfeldt, 'Israelitisch-jüdische Religionsgeschichte und alttestamentliche Theologie', *ZAW* 44 (1926), pp. 1-12.

3. W. Eichrodt, *Theologie des Alten Testaments*, I-III (1933-1939; ET, *Theology of the Old Testament*, I-II, 1961-1967).

4. Eichrodt, *Theologie*, I, pp. 2-5; cf. *Theology*, I, pp. 27-31.

5. O. Procksch, *Theologie des Alten Testaments* (1950), pp. 1-47.

6. M. Noth, 'Die Vergegenwärtigung des Alten Testaments in der Verkündigung', *EvTh* 12 (1952/53), pp. 6-17 (= C. Westermann, *Probleme alttestamentlicher Hermeneutik* [1960], pp. 54-68; ET, C. Westermann, *Essays on Old Testament Interpretation* [1963], pp. 76-88 = *Interpretation* 15 [1961], pp. 50-60).

7. G. von Rad, 'Typologische Auslegung des Alten Testaments', *EvTh* 12 (1952/53), pp. 17-33 (ET, Westermann, *Essays*, pp. 17-39 = *Interpretation* 15 [1961], pp. 174-92).

8. W. Zimmerli, 'Verheissung und Erfüllung', *EvTh* 12 (1952/53), pp. 34-59 (= Westermann, *Probleme*, pp. 69-101; ET, Westermann, *Essays*, pp. 89-122 = *Interpretation* 15 [1961], pp. 310-38).

9. H.-J. Kraus, 'Gespräch mit Martin Buber', *EvTh* 12 (1952/53), pp. 59-77.

10. H.W. Wolff, 'Der grosse Jesreeltag (Hosea 2,13)', *EvTh* 12 (1952/53), pp. 78-104.

11. F. Baumgärtel, *Die Bedeutung des Alten Testaments für den Christen* (1925); *Ist die Kritik am Alten Testament berechtigt?* (1927); *Die Eigenart der alttestamentlichen Frömmigkeit* (1932).

12. Baumgärtel, 'Erwägungen zur Darstellung der Theologie des Alten Testaments', *ThLZ* 76 (1951), pp. 257-72.

13. Baumgärtel, *Verheissung. Zur Frage des evangelischen Verständnisses des Alten Testaments* (1952), pp. 106-27.

14. Baumgärtel, 'Ohne Schlüssel vor der Tür des Wortes Gottes?' *EvTh* 13 (1953), pp. 413-21; 'Der Dissensus im Verständnis des Alten Testaments', *EvTh* 14 (1954), pp. 298-313; von Rad, 'Verheissung', *EvTh* 13 (1953), pp. 406-13; Wolff, 'Zur Hermeneutik des Alten Testaments', *EvTh* 16 (1956), pp. 337-70 (= Westermann, *Probleme*, pp. 140-80; ET, Westermann, *Essays*,

pp. 160-99 = Interpretation 15 [1961], pp. 439-72). Cf. the survey by L. Schmidt, 'Die Einheit zwischen Altem und Neuem Testament im Streit zwischen Friedrich Baumgärtel und Gerhard von Rad', *EvTh* 35 (1975), pp. 119-39.

15. A.A. van Ruler, *Die christliche Kirche und das Alte Testament* (BEvTh, 23; 1955).

16. Baumgärtel, 'Erwägungen', pp. 268-70.

17. A. Jepsen, 'Probleme der Auslegung des Alten Testaments', *ZSTh* 23 (1954), pp. 373-86; Eichrodt, 'Ist die typologische Exegese sachgemässe Exegese?', *ThLZ* 81 (1956), pp. 641-54 (= *VTS* 4 [1957], pp. 161-80 = Westermann, *Probleme*, pp. 205-26; ET, Westermann, *Essays*, pp. 224-45).

18. Eichrodt, *ThLZ* 81 (1956), pp. 652f; *Essays*, pp. 244f.

19. For a survey of the Biblical Theology Movement, see B.S. Childs, *Biblical Theology in Crisis* (1970), pp. 13-50. Cf. also J. Barr, 'Biblical Theology', *IDB Supplementary Volume* (1976), pp. 105f.

20. G.E. Wright, *God Who Acts* (SBT, 8; 1952).

21. See e.g. the quotation from Eichrodt *ibid.*, pp. 43f. and the references to Noth and von Rad, *ibid.*, p. 45 n.1, p. 52 n.1, pp. 70-77, etc.

22. Wright's book does contain some peculiarities. The reader wonders whether Wright could really have believed that the words of Johann Gerhard, quoted on p. 61, were 'written in 1762'. The quotation is taken over from L. Goppelt, *Typos* (1939), p. 8 n. 2, where Gerhard is quoted according to the Cotta-*edition* of 1762! (Gerhard's *Loci Theologici*, a major work of early Lutheran Orthodoxy, originally appeared 1610-1622).

23. E. Jacob, *Théologie de l'Ancien Testament* (1955); ET, *Theology of the Old Testament* (3rd edn; 1964).

24. Th. C. Vriezen, *Theologie des Alten Testaments in Grundzügen* (1956); ET, *An Outline of Old Testament Theology* (2nd edn; 1970).

25. G. von Rad, *Theologie des Alten Testaments*. I. *Die Theologie der geschichtlichen Überlieferungen Israels* (1957). II. *Die Theologie der prophetischen Überlieferungen Israels* (1961); ET, *Old Testament Theology*, I. *The Theology of Israel's Historical Traditions* (1962); II. *The Theology of Israel's Prophetic Traditions* (1965).

26. Baumgärtel, 'Gerhard von Rads "Theologie des Alten Testaments"', *ThLZ* 86 (1961), pp. 801-16, 895-908.

27. Von Rad, in the preface of the 4th German edition of his *Theologie*, declared that he would not respond to Baumgärtel's criticisms, since there were obviously no possibilities of a meaningful discussion (von Rad, *Theologie des Alten Testaments*, I [6th edn; 1969] p. 13).

28. F. Hesse, 'Die Erforschung der Geschichte Israels als theologische Aufgabe', *KuD* 4 (1958), pp. 1-19; 'Kerygma oder geschichtliche Wirklichkeit?', *ZThK* 57 (1960), pp. 17-26.

29. H. Graf Reventlow, 'Grundfragen der alttestamentlichen Theologie im Lichte der neueren deutschen Forschung', *ThZ* 17 (1961), pp. 81-98.

30. M. Honecker, 'Zum Verständnis der Geschichte in Gerhard von Rads Theologie des Alten Testaments', *EvTh* 23 (1963), pp. 143-68.

31. H. Conzelmann, 'Fragen an Gerhard von Rad', *EvTh* 24 (1964), pp. 113-25.

32. W. Pannenberg, *Offenbarung als Geschichte* (KuD, Beiheft 1; 1961); ET, *Revelation as History* (1969).

33. R. Rendtorff, 'Die Offenbarungsvorstellungen im Alten Israel', in Pannenberg, *Offenbarung als Geschichte*, pp. 21-41 (ET, Pannenberg, *Revelation as History*, pp. 23-53); '"Offenbarung" im Alten Testament', *ThLZ* 85 (1960), pp. 833-38; 'Geschichte und Wort im Alten Testament', *EvTh* 22 (1962), pp. 621-649.

34. Zimmerli, '"Offenbarung" im Alten Testament', *EvTh* 22 (1962), pp. 15-31.

35. K. Koch, 'Der Tod des Religionsstifters', *KuD* 8 (1962), pp. 100-23.

36. Baumgärtel, 'Der Tod des Religionsstifters', *KuD* 9 (1963), pp. 223-33; 'Das Offenbarungszeugnis des Alten Testaments im Lichte der religionsgeschichtlich-vergleichenden Forschung', *ZThK* 64 (1967), pp. 393-422.

37. F. Mildenberger, *Gottes Tat im Wort* (1964).

38. Hesse, *Das Alte Testament als Buch der Kirche* (1966). See also his 'Zur Frage der Wertung und der Geltung alttestamentlicher Texte', in Westermann, *Probleme*, pp. 266-94 (ET, Westermann, *Essays*, pp. 285-313).

39. Hesse, *Abschied von der Heilsgeschichte* (ThSt, 108; 1971).

40. James Barr's penetrating criticism of the 'Biblical Theology' positions (Barr, *The Semantics of Biblical Language* [1961]; *Old and New in Interpretation* [1966]) played an important part in this.

41. See Childs, *Biblical Theology in Crisis* (1970), pp. 61-87.

42. H.W. Wolff, *Probleme biblischer Theologie* (1971).

43. L. Perlitt, *Bundestheologie im Alten Testament* (WMANT, 36; 1969).

44. Rendtorff, *Das überlieferungsgeschichtliche Problem des Pentateuch* (BZAW, 147; 1977).

45. H.H. Schmid, *Der sogenannte Jahwist* (1976).

46. Cf. E. Nielsen, 'The traditio-historical study of the Pentateuch', Nielsen, *Law, History, and Tradition* (1983), pp. 149-153 (= K. Jeppesen and B. Otzen, *The Productions of Time* [1984], pp. 24-28).

47. Von Rad, *Weisheit in Israel* (1970); ET, *Wisdom in Israel* (1972).

48. See Schmid, *Altorientalische Welt in der alttestamentlichen Theologie* (1974).

49. Childs, *Biblical Theology in Crisis* (1970).

50. Kraus, *Die biblische Theologie. Ihre Geschichte und Problematik* (1970).

51. See, among numerous publications on this theme, Barr, 'Trends and Prospects in Biblical Theology', *JTS* 25 (1974), pp. 265-82; 'Biblical Theology', *IDB Supplementary Volume* (1976), pp. 104-11; E. Jacob, 'De la

théologie de l'Ancien Testament à la théologie biblique', *RHPhR* 57 (1977), pp. 513-18; S. Wagner, '"Biblische Theologien" und "Biblische Theologie"', *ThLZ* 103 (1978), pp. 785-98; A.H.J. Gunneweg, '"Theologie des Alten Testaments" oder "Biblische Theologie"?', A.H.J. Gunneweg and O. Kaiser, *Testgemäss* (1979), pp. 39-46.

    52. See G. Ebeling, 'The Meaning of "Biblical Theology"', *JTS* 6 (1955), pp. 210-25 (= *Word and Faith* [1963], pp. 79-97).

    53. H. Gese, *Vom Sinai zum Zion* (BEvTh, 64; 1974); *Zur biblischen Theologie* (*BEvTh*, 78; 1977).

    54. R. Smend, *Die Mitte des Alten Testaments* (ThSt, 101; 1970).

    55. Zimmerli, 'Zum Problem der "Mitte des Alten Testaments"', *EvTh* 35 (1975), pp. 97-118.

    56. See E. Käsemann, *Das Neue Testament als Kanon* (1970).

    57. Childs, *Introduction to the Old Testament as Scripture* (1979).

    58. Barr, 'Childs' Introduction to the Old Testament as Scripture', *JSOT* 16 (1980), pp. 12-23; *Holy Scripture. Canon, Authority, Criticism* (1983).

    59. See J.I. Jensen, 'Literaturkritische Herausforderungen an die Theologie', *EvTh* 41 (1981), pp. 377-401.

    60. Cf. G. Hasel, 'A Decade of OT Theology: Retrospect and Prospect', *ZAW* 93 (1981), pp. 165-83.

    61. G. Fohrer, *Theologische Grundstrukturen des Alten Testaments* (1972).

    62. Zimmerli, *Grundriss der alttestamentlichen Theologie* (1972) (ET, *Old Testament Theology in Outline* [1978]). Cf. also his 'Erwägungen zur Gestalt einer alttestamentlichen Theologie', *ThLZ* 98 (1973), pp. 81-98.

    63. R.E. Clements, *Old Testament Theology. A Fresh Approach* (1978).

    64. C. Westermann, *Theologie des Alten Testaments in Grundzügen* (1978) (ET, *Elements of Old Testament Theology* [1982]).

Notes to Chapter 2

    1. J.Ph. Gabler, 'De iusto discrimine theologiae biblicae et dogmaticae regundisque recte utriusque finibus', *Opuscula academica, Kleinere theologische Schriften*, II, pp. 179-98.

    2. Procksch, *Theologie des Alten Testaments* (1950), pp. 12f.

    3. *Ibid.*, p. 13 n. 1.

    4. 'Alle Theologie ist Christologie. Jesus Christus ist die einzige Gestalt unserer Erfahrungswelt, in der Gottes Offenbarung vollständig ist. Gott ist in Christus und Christus in Gott, dies Verhältnis zwischen Gott und Mensch ist völlig einzigartig in der Geschichte; es wiederholt sich in keiner andern Gestalt' (*ibid.*, p. 1).

    5. *Ibid.*, pp. 1f.

    6. *Ibid.*, pp. 2-7.

    7. In a footnote (*ibid.*, p. 44 n. 2) Procksch informs us that the expression

'theology of history' ('Theologie der Geschichte') is borrowed from P. Wapler's biography *Johannes von Hofmann* (1914). Clearly Procksch sees his work as standing in continuity with important lines in Hofmann's theology. The idea of history as an organic whole with Christ as the centre obviously has its background here.

8. Procksch, *ibid.*, pp. 7f.
9. *Ibid.*, pp. 10-12.
10. *Ibid.*, p. 13.
11. *Ibid.*, pp. 13f.
12. *Ibid.*, pp. 14f.
13. *Ibid.*, pp. 15f.
14. 'Freilich ist der Schatz des alttestamentlichen wie des neutestamentlichen Glaubenslebens überall in irdischen Gefässen enthalten. Es sind die Schalen der Religionsgeschichte, aber nicht ihr Kern, wenn wir auf fremde mythologische oder kultische Vorstellungen stossen, in denen sich das geschichtliche Leben entfaltet hat . . . So wird innerhalb der Theologie der Religionsgeschichte volles Recht widerfahren; sie ist die Form, in der der Glaubensinhalt fassbar wird' (*ibid.*, pp. 17f.).
15. *Ibid.*, pp. 18f.
16. Kraus, *Die biblische Theologie*, p. 129.
17. Procksch, *Theologie*, p. 33. M. Luther, *Operationes in Psalmos* (1519-1527), *WA*, V, p. 571.
18. G. von Rad, *Theologie des Alten Testaments*, I (6th edn; 1969), pp. 117-42 (ET, *Old Testament Theology*, I [1962], pp. 105-28).
19. *Theology*, I, pp. 105f.
20. *Ibid.*, p. 111.
21. *Ibid.*, p. 106.
22. *Ibid.*, p. 115.
23. *Ibid.*, p. 116.
24. *Ibid.*, pp. 116f.
25. *Ibid.*, p. 118.
26. *Ibid.*, p. 119.
27. *Ibid.*
28. *Ibid.*, p. 121.
29. Cf. von Rad's own statement in the preface (*ibid.*, p. v).
30. C.A. Keller, *ThZ* 14 (1958), p. 308.
31. *Ibid.*, pp. 308f.
32. *Ibid.*, p. 308.
33. F. Hesse, 'Kerygma oder geschichtliche Wirklichkeit?', *ZThK* 57 (1960), pp. 17-26.
34. *Ibid.*, p. 19.
35. *Ibid.*, pp. 20f.
36. *Ibid.*, pp. 20-23. Hesse acknowledges his debt to Baumgärtel—see Hesse, *ibid.*, p. 23 n. 1 and p. 26 n. 1. See the section on Baumgärtel's

hermeneutics below, pp. 52-59.

37. F. Baumgärtel, 'Gerhard von Rads "Theologie des Alten Testaments"', *ThLZ* 86 (1961), pp. 801-16, 895-908.

38. *Ibid.*, pp. 803f.

39. *Ibid.*, p. 806.

40. Von Rad, *Theology*, I, p. 121.

41. Baumgärtel, *ThLZ* 86 (1961), p. 903.

42. Eichrodt, *Theologie des Alten Testaments*, I (1933), pp. 6-26 (ET, *Theology of the Old Testament*, I [1961], pp. 36-69).

43. Vriezen, *An Outline of Old Testament Theology* (2nd edn: 1970), p. 157.

44. *Ibid.*, p. 175.

45. *Ibid.*, p. 170. The 'communion' idea is given more emphasis, and the arrangement is more strictly systematic in Vriezen's second English edition than in previous German editions. The second English edition is based on the third Dutch edition. See *An Outline*, preface, p. 7.

46. Von Rad, *Theologie*, I, p. 128; *Theology*, I, p. 115.

47. Von Rad, 'Offene Fragen im Umkreis einer Theologie des Alten Testaments', *ThLZ* 88 (1963), p.405; cf. *Old Testament Theology*, II (1965), p. 414.

48. As suggested by Reventlow, 'Grundfragen', *ThZ* 17 (1961), p. 96.

49. Von Rad, 'Offene Fragen', p. 405.

50. *Ibid*, p. 416; *Theologie des Alten Testaments*, II (5th edn; 1968), p. 447; *Old Testament Theology*, II (1962), p. 428.

51. 'Offene Fragen', p. 416; *Theologie*, II, p. 447, cf. *ibid*, pp. 380f; cf. *Theology*, II, pp. 414, 416.

52. *Theologie*, I, p. 356; *Theology*, I, p. 344.

53. Honecker, 'Zum Verständnis der Geschichte', *EvTh* 23 (1963), pp. 144-48; G.F. Hasel, *Old Testament Theology. Basic Issues in the Current Debate* (2nd edn; 1975), pp. 85-88.

54. S. Herrmann, 'Die konstruktive Restauration', in H.W. Wolff, *Probleme biblischer Theologie* (1971), p. 167.

55. *Ibid.*, p. 168.

56. Smend, *Die Mitte des Alten Testaments* (ThSt 101; 1970), p. 21.

57. *Ibid.*, p. 48.

58. *Ibid.*, pp. 48f.

59. See *ibid.*, p. 48 n. 203.

60. Fohrer, *Theologische Grundstrukturen des Alten Testaments* (1972), p. 98.

61. Hasel, 'The Problem of the Center in the OT Theology Debate', *ZAW* 86 (1974), pp. 79f.

62. *Ibid.*, pp. 81f.; *Old Testament Theology. Basic Issues*, pp. 102, 138f.

63. Hasel, 'The Problem', p. 81.

64. Zimmerli, 'Zum Problem der "Mitte des Alten Testaments"', *EvTh* 35

(1975), p. 102.
 65. *Ibid.*, p. 108.
 66. *Ibid.*, pp. 104-109.
 67. *Ibid.*, p. 111.
 68. *Ibid.*, pp. 115-17.
 69. 'Die Frage nach der Mitte des Alten Testaments führte ... auf die Frage nach jenem perspektivischen Fluchtpunkt, der nicht auf der Oberfläche des Bildes zu greifen ist, sondern hinter ihr liegt, auf den hin aber alles, was auf der Oberfläche des Bildes zu erkennen ist, bezogen bleibt. Das Bild hat sich darin als unsachgemäss erwiesen, als es sich nicht um die Erforschung eines ruhenden Punktes hinter den Einzelheiten des Bildes geht, sondern um einen gebietenden Herrn, der in Angriff und Forderung aber zugleich in barmherziger Hinwendung zu seinem Volk und seiner Kreatur auf diese zugeht' (*ibid.*, p. 117).
 70. *Ibid.*, p. 188.
 71. Von Rad, *Das formgeschichtliche Problem des Hexateuch* (BWANT, 78; 1938), p. 2; cf. 'The Form-Critical Problem of the Hexateuch', *The Problem of the Hexateuch* (1965), p. 2.
 72. See Conzelmann, 'Fragen an Gerhard von Rad', *EvTh* 24 (1964), p. 113; Smend, *Mitte*, pp. 23f.; Zimmerli, 'Zum Problem', p. 99.
 73. The image is partly borrowed from von Rad, *Theologie*, II, p. 446; cf. *Theology*, II, p. 427.
 74. Von Rad, *Das formgeschichtliche Problem des Hexateuch* (BWANT, 78; 1938) (ET, 'The Form-Critical Problem of the Hexateuch', *The Problem of the Hexateuch* [1965], pp. 1-78).
 75. *Theologie*, I, p. 118; (ET I, p. 106).
 76. *Theologie*, II, pp. 339-41; (ET II, pp. 319-21).
 77. *Theologie*, II, pp. 342f; (ET II, pp. 322f.).
 78. Cf. Zimmerli, *VT* 13 (1963), pp. 100f. As observed above, certain critics have seen in Deuteronomistic theology the 'secret centre' in von Rad's OT theology.
 79. *Theologie*, II, pp. 124-27, 182-94; (ET, II, pp. 115-18, 176-87).
 80. *Theologie*, II, p. 344; (ET II, p. 323).
 81. *Theologie*, II, pp. 344-46; (ET II, pp. 323-25).
 82. *Theologie*, II, pp. 342-49; (ET II, pp. 322-28).
 83. *Theologie*, II, p.353; (ET II, pp. 332f.).
 84. *Theologie*, II, pp. 360-77; (ET II, pp. 338-54).
 85. *Theologie*, II, pp. 377f.; (ET II, pp. 355f.).
 86. *Theologie*, II, pp. 380-407; (ET II, pp. 357-82).
 87. *Theologie*, II, p. 410; (ET II, p. 385).
 88. *Theologie*, II, pp. 407-12; (ET II, pp. 382-87).
 89. See L. Rost, 'Das kleine geschichtliche Credo', *Das kleine Credo und andere Studien* (1965), pp. 11-25.
 90. See Schmid, *Der sogenannte Jahwist* (1976); Rose, *Deuteronomist und*

120   *Problems and Prospects of Old Testament Theology*

Jahwist (AThANT 67; 1981).

91. See Rendtorff, *Das überlieferungsgeschichtliche Problem des Pentateuch* (BZAW, 147; 1977).

92. Honecker, 'Zum Verständnis der Geschichte', *EvTh* 23 (1963), pp. 143-68. H. Conzelmann, in an equally critical essay on von Rad's OT theology (*EvTh* 24 (1964), pp. 113-25), quotes the following remark from Luther's commentary on Galatians (to Gal. 4.4): 'Non enim tempus fecit filium mitti, sed econtra missio filii fecit tempus plenitudinis' (*WA*, LVII [Galaterbrief], p. 30), and adds that all critical questions to von Rad are contained *in nuce* in this sentence. In fact, the relationship between promise and fulfilment is not a 'linear', but a 'dialectical' one, Conzelmann states with a somewhat slogan-like expression (*EvTh* 24 [1964], p. 125).

93. Von Rad, 'Antwort auf Conzelmanns Fragen', *EvTh* 24 (1964), p. 391.

94. Conzelmann, 'Fragen', p. 117.

95. Rendtorff, 'Hermeneutik des Alten Testaments', *ZThK* 57 (1960), p. 33.

96. H. Gese, 'Erwägungen zur Einheit der biblischen Theologie', *ZThK* 67 (1970), pp. 417-36 (= Gese, *Vom Sinai zum Zion* [1974], pp. 11-30).

97. 'Wir kommen zu der These: Das Alte Testament entsteht durch das Neue Testament; das Neue Testament bildet den Abschluss eines Traditionsprozesses, der wesentlich eine Einheit, ein Kontinuum ist' (*ibid.*, p. 420).

98. *Ibid.*, pp. 422f.

99. *Ibid.*, p. 424.

100. *Ibid.*, p. 425.

101. *Ibid.*, pp. 424f.

102. 'Die Geschichte der Traditionsbildung ist in gewisser Weise eine Geschichte des die Offenbarung erfahrenden Bewusstseins, an dem sich eine ungeheure Aufweitung des Wirklichkeitsfeldes vollzieht' (*ibid.*, p. 429).

103. *Ibid.*, pp. 435f.

104. Cf. H.-J. Kraus, 'Theologie als Traditionsbildung?' *Biblische Theologie heute* (1977), pp. 66-68.

105. R. Bultmann, 'Weissagung und Erfüllung', *StTh* 2 (1948), pp. 21-44 (= *ZThK* 47 [1950], pp. 360-83 = *Glauben und Verstehen*, II [1952], pp. 162-86 = Westermann, *Probleme*, pp. 28-53; ET, Bultmann, *Essays Philosophical and Theological* [1955], pp. 182-208 = Westermann, *Essays*, pp. 50-75). See also Bultmann's earlier essay 'Die Bedeutung des Alten Testaments für den christlichen Glauben', *Glauben und Verstehen*, I (1933), pp. 313-36 (ET, Anderson, *The Old Testament and Christian Faith* [1964], pp. 8-35).

106. *StTh* 2 (1948), pp. 21-26 (ET, Westermann, *Essays*, pp. 50-55).

107. *StTh* 2 (1948), pp. 27-29 (ET, pp. 55-58).

108. *StTh* 2 (1948), p. 29 (ET, p. 58).

109. *StTh* 2 (1948), pp. 30-42 (ET, pp. 59-72).

110. Westermann, *Essays*, p. 73.

111. *Ibid.*

112. *Ibid.*

113. *StTh* 2 (1948), pp. 43f. (ET, pp. 74f.).
114. Westermann, *Essays*, p. 75.
115. Baumgärtel, 'The Hermeneutical Problem of the Old Testament', Westermann, *Essays*, p. 145.
116. Baumgärtel, *Verheissung* (1952), pp. 7-16.
117. *Ibid.*, p. 11.
118. 'Die Verheissung im evangelischen Sinn als Verheissung in Christus hat eine Beziehung zum Alten Testament, sie umschliesst die Verheissung des Alten Testaments' (*ibid.*, pp. 14f.).
119. *Ibid.*, pp. 11-14.
120. *Ibid.*, p. 8.
121. *Ibid.*, pp. 9f.
122. 'Nur in der Busse wird die Verheissung in Christus an mir faktisch' (*ibid.*, p. 10).
123. *Ibid.*, pp. 15f.
124. *Ibid.*, pp. 16-27.
125. 'Dann ist letztlich die Verheissung in Christus, in der Gott von uns Christen ebenfalls als der aus freier Gnade schenkende begriffen wird, als der, der uns in seine Lebensgemeinschaft hineinziehen will als der Herr, doch im Zusammenhang mit dem *Grund* aller Verheissungen im Alten Testament, mit der *Grundverheissung an Israel: "Ich bin der Herr dein Gott"*' (*ibid.*, p. 19).
126. *Ibid.*, p. 49.
127. *Ibid.*, p. 25.
128. 'The Hermeneutical Problem', *Essays*, p. 152.
129. *Verheissung*, p. 47.
130. *Ibid.*, pp. 38f.
131. 'The Hermeneutical Problem', *Essays*, p. 151.
132. *Verheissung*, pp. 47f.
133. *Ibid.*, p. 51.
134. *Ibid.*, pp. 53-56, 64-67.
135. *Essays*, p. 154.
136. *Ibid.*, p. 156.
137. See the references in *Verheissung*, p. 37 nn. 25-28, p. 53 nn. 33-35, p. 57 n. 40, p. 69 n. 50, etc.
138. Luther's theological position is expressed with particular clarity in some of his disputations. See, above all, the disputations against the 'antinomists' (1537-1540), *WA*, XXXIX/1, pp. 334-584, *WA*, XXXIX/2, pp. 122-44.
139. *Essays*, p.135.
140. *Ibid.*
141. See Baumgärtel, 'Erwägungen', *ThLZ* 76 (1951), p. 259.
142. Von Rad, *Theologie*, II, pp. 108-21 (ET II, pp. 99-112).
143. *Theologie*, II, pp. 119-21 (ET II, pp. 110-12).

144.   *Theologie*, I, pp. 118-20 (ET I, pp. 106-108).

145.   *Theology*, I, p. 108.

146.   *Theologie*, I, pp. 120-24 (ET I, pp. 108-11).

147.   'Offene Fragen', *ThLZ* 88 (1963), p. 409. Cf. *Theology*, II, p. 418. The 'Postscript' of *Theology*, II, pp. 410ff., is largely based upon von Rad's essay in *ThLZ* 88 (1963), pp. 401-18.

148.   Thus von Rad says with a formulation that would seem consciously to avoid taking a stand, 'A question which will occupy theologians for a long time to come is whether it is still possible to say that each view is of equal value in considering the phenomenon of Israel's history in its various conceptions, or whether nowadays we must choose between them' (*Theology*, II, p. 418).

149.   *Theologie*, II, p.443 (cf. ET II, pp. 422-25).

150.   See *Theologie*, II, pp. 442-46 (ET II, pp. 425-27).

151.   Cf. *Theologie*, II, p.444 (ET II, p. 427).

152.   Hesse, 'Die Erforschung', *KuD* 4 (1958), p. 7.

153.   *Ibid.*, pp. 1f.

154.   *Ibid.*, pp. 3-8.

155.   *Ibid.*, pp. 9-11.

156.   *Ibid.*, pp. 2, 19.

157.   Rendtorff, 'Hermeneutik', *ZThK* 57 (1960), pp. 27-40; 'Geschichte und Überlieferung', *Studien zur Theologie der alttestamentlichen Überlieferungen* (1961), pp. 81-94.

158.   Rendtorff, 'Hermeneutik', pp. 36f.

159.   *Ibid.*, pp. 38f.

160.   *Ibid.*, p. 39.

161.   'Geschichte und Überlieferung', pp. 84-88.

162.   'Hermeneutik', p. 39.

163.   'Hermeneutik', pp. 39f.; 'Geschichte und Überlieferung', pp. 89-91.

164.   'Hermeneutik', p. 40; 'Geschichte und Überlieferung', p. 94.

165.   'Geschichte und Überlieferung', p. 94 n. 39, with reference to W. Pannenberg, *KuD* 5 (1959), pp. 218-37, 259-88.

166.   Cf. Hesse's statement, 'Mit von Rads Buch ist die kerygmatische Theologie nun mit voller Wucht auch in den alttestamentlichen Bereich eingebrochen', 'Kerygma', *ZThK* 57 (1960), p. 21.

167.   See Pannenberg, 'Kerygma und Geschichte', *Studien zur Theologie der alttestamentlichen Überlieferungen* (1961), pp. 134-39 (ET, Pannenberg, *Basic Questions in Theology*, I [1970], pp. 81-95); 'Glaube und Wirklichkeit im Denken Gerhard von Rads', *Gerhard von Rad. Seine Bedeutung für die Theologie* (1973), pp. 37-54.

168.   Baumgärtel, 'Das alttestamentliche Geschehen als "heilsgeschicht-liches" Geschehen', *Geschichte und Altes Testament* (BHTh, 16; 1953), pp. 13-28.

169.   'Der, der glaubt, erfährt unter der Botschaft vom Geschehen

Christus seine Fragwürdigkeit im Angesicht Gottes und die Rettung (σωτηρία) aus seiner Ausweglosigkeit vor Gott. *Das ist die Heilsgeschichte: das Wort ward Fleisch.* Dies Geschehen wird uns zum heilsgeschichtlichen Geschehen, indem beim glaubenden Aufnehmen seiner Bezeugung, das Heil (Sündenvergebung, Kindschaft, ewiges Leben—Rechtfertigung) als faktisch an uns, als unsere Existenz gründend, von uns erfahren wird' (*ibid.*, pp. 14f.).

170. *Ibid.*, p. 16.

171. *Ibid.*, pp. 18f.

172. *Ibid.*, p. 20.

173. *Ibid.*, p. 21.

174. *Ibid.*

175. See Hesse, *Das Alte Testament als Buch der Kirche* (1966).

176. Hesse, *Abschied von der Heilsgeschichte* (ThSt, 108; 1971).

177. *Ibid.*, pp. 7f.

178. *Ibid.*, pp. 17f.

179. *Ibid.*, pp. 19f.

180. *Ibid.*, pp. 20-23, 31.

181. *Ibid.*, pp. 25-30.

182. *Ibid.*, pp. 31-35.

183. *Ibid.*, p. 37.

184. *Ibid.*, pp. 38-40.

185. *Ibid.*, pp. 40f.

186. *Ibid.*, pp. 41-43. 'Die These, Geschichte habe von Gott her einen bestimmten Sinn, und dieser sei nur dem glaubenden Menschen zugänglich, ist möglich. Aber man kann nicht behaupten, in, mit und unter der kontinuierlichen Geschehensabfolge, die jedermann einsichtig ist, ereigne sich ein anderer kontinuierlicher Geschehenszusammenhang, der sich nur dem glaubenden Menschen eröffnet' (*ibid.*, p. 43).

187. 'Die Frage der Kontinuität', *ibid.*, pp. 49-67.

188. *Ibid.*, pp. 49-52.

189. *Ibid.*, pp. 53f. 'Gottes ist nicht das kontinuierliche, sondern das kontingente Handeln. Zugespitzt formuliert: Wo Gott richtend und rettend eingreift, da kann es Geschichte im Sinne eines kontinuierlichen Geschehenszusammenhangs gar nicht geben' (*ibid.*, p. 54).

190. *Ibid.*, pp. 55-59.

191. *Ibid.*, p. 58.

192. *Ibid.*, pp. 59-66.

193. *Ibid.*, pp. 66f.

194. See *ibid.*, pp. 32-33 nn. 33-35, p. 64 nn. 54-56, p. 65 nn. 58-59, 61.

195. Baumgärtel, *ThLZ* 86 (1961), pp. 812, 895-901.

196. This implicit premiss in von Rad's work is the source of a certain confusion, partly increased by von Rad's sometimes rather imprecise language. Often von Rad speaks of 'Israel's testimonies' or 'Israel's

confessions' in a way that may give the impression that it is 'Israel' which possesses a particular authority. However, it is undoubtedly more natural to interpret von Rad as I have attempted above. Then, the authority belongs to the OT texts themselves. And after all, according to von Rad these texts are the immediate products of 'Israel's confessions'.

197. B.S. Childs, *Biblical Theology in Crisis* (1970), p. 99.
198. *Ibid.*, pp. 97f.
199. *Ibid.*, pp. 99f.
200. *Ibid.*, p. 104.
201. *Ibid.*, pp. 111-13.
202. Childs, *Introduction to the Old Testament as Scripture* (1979). Childs applies similar viewpoints to the NT canon in his *The New Testament as Canon: An Introduction* (1984).
203. *Introduction to the Old Testament as Scripture*, pp. 61f.
204. *Ibid.*, p. 78.
205. *Ibid.*
206. *Ibid.*, p. 41, cf. p. 78.
207. *Ibid.*, pp. 73-75.
208. *Ibid.*, p. 326.
209. Barr, 'Childs' Introduction to the Old Testament as Scripture', *JSOT* 16 (1980), pp. 12-23; *Holy Scripture* (1983).
210. *Holy Scripture*, p. 75, cf. p. 49.
211. *Ibid.*, pp. 75-77.
212. *Ibid.*, pp. 80f.
213. *Ibid.*, pp. 50f.
214. *Ibid.*, pp. 83f.
215. *Ibid.*, pp. 84-90.
216. *Ibid.*, pp. 92f.
217. *Ibid.*, pp. 93f.
218. *Ibid.*, p. 67, cf. pp. 96-99.
219. Cf. *ibid.*, pp. 136f.
220. Cf. *ibid.*, p. 102. An incisive critique of Childs's position is also to be found in J. Barton, *Reading the Old Testament* (1984), pp. 77-103.
221. See G. Ebeling, 'The Meaning of "Biblical Theology"', *JTS* 6 (1955), pp. 216f.; Kraus, *Die biblische Theologie*, pp. 19-30.
222. J.Ph. Gabler, *Opuscula academica, Kleinere theologische Schriften*, II (1831), pp. 179-98. Cf. also R. Smend, 'Johann Philipp Gablers Begründung der biblischen Theologie', *EvTh* 22 (1962), pp. 345-57; J. Sandys-Wunsch and L. Eldredge, 'J.P. Gabler and the Distinction between Biblical and Dogmatic Theology', *SJT* 33 (1980), pp. 133-58.
223. G. Ebeling, 'The Meaning of "Biblical Theology"', *JTS* 6 (1955), pp. 210-25.
224. *Ibid.*, p. 210.
225. *Ibid.*, pp. 211-13.

226. *Ibid.*, pp. 213-16.
227. *Ibid.*, pp. 216f.
228. *Ibid.*, pp. 218-20.
229. *Ibid.*, pp. 220-22.
230. *Ibid.*, pp. 222f.
231. *Ibid.*, p. 224.
232. Kraus, *Die biblische Theologie* (1970).
233. Childs, *Biblical Theology in Crisis* (1970).
234. 'Sollte es gelingen, in dieser Sache erste Schritte zu tun, erste Projekte in Angriff zu nehmen und erste Entwürfe vorzulegen, dann wären die förderlichen Auswirkungen auf das Ganze der theologischen Wissenschaft kaum abzusehen und gewiss nicht zu überschätzen' (Kraus, *Biblische Theologie*, p. v).
235. Childs, *Biblical Theology*, pp. 91-96.
236. Kraus, *Biblische Theologie*, pp. 335f. (with reference to K. Barth, *Die Kirchliche Dogmatik*, I, 2, p. 457).
237. Kraus, *ibid.*, p. 346 (with reference to K. Barth, *Einführung in die evangelische Theologie* [1962], p. 53).
238. See above pp. 68-70.
239. Kraus, *Biblische Theologie*, pp. 369-71; Childs, *Biblical Theology*, pp. 111-12.
240. Kraus, *ibid.*, pp. 371-80.
241. Childs, *ibid.*, pp. 114-18.

Notes to Chapter 3

1. This point is made by Barr, *Holy Scripture*, p. 49 n. 1.
2. See Luther, *Kirchenpostille* (1522), *WA*, X/1, 1. Hälfte, p. 17, 4-12; *Epistel St. Petri gepredigt und ausgelegt* (1523), *WA*, XII, p. 275. See also the fine observations by H. Bornkamm, *Luther und das Alte Testament* (1948), pp. 69-74.
3. Here, perhaps, a justified intention may be acknowledged in the tradition-historical conception of H. Gese. The early Christians, participating in an ongoing tradition-historical process, took over the Jewish traditions embodied in the OT. See above pp. 49-50.
4. The fact that biblical criticism is in this important sense a true heir of the Reformation, is emphasized by G. Ebeling, 'Die Bedeutung der historisch-kritischen Methode für die protestantische Theologie und Kirche', *Wort und Glaube* (2nd edn; 1962), pp. 1-49 (ET, *Word and Faith* [1963], pp. 17-61). The same point is made by Barr, *The Scope and Authority of the Bible* (Explorations in Theology, 7, 1980), p. 78.
5. H.W. Wolff, 'Zur Hermeneutik des Alten Testaments', *EvTh* 16 (1956), pp. 343-46 (= Westermann, *Probleme* [1960], pp. 147-50; ET,

Interpretation 15 [1961], pp. 445-47 = Westermann, *Essays*, pp. 167-70).

6. 'In his essence, Yahweh is not a figure of mythology in the sense that one could speak of him in the manner of the myths of the neighbouring lands, which chatter so much of the 'private life' of their gods and of their life together in the pantheon' (*Essays*, p. 168 [with reference (n. 23) to the Utnapishtim story in the Gilgamesh Epic]). In a proper religion-historical perspective, the myths of the ancient Near East do not 'chatter' about the private life of their gods.

7. *Essays*, pp. 168-69.

8. *Ibid.*, p. 170.

9. Cf. the very appropriate remarks by E. Gerstenberger, *Wesen und Herkunft des 'apodiktischen Rechts'* (WMANT, 20; 1965), pp. 15f.

10. Wilhelm Vischer, *Das Christuszeugnis des Alten Testaments* I (1934), II (1942).

11. 'Tota scriptura eo tendit, ut Christum nobis propanat cognoscendum, hic universae scripturae scopus est, per hunc demum nobis ad patrem aditus paratur' (Luther, *In Genesin Declarationes* [1527], *WA*, XXIV, p. 16).

12. If there is in fact such a relation between the Old Testament and the ministry of Christ, then a historical-critical reading of the Old Testament may in a certain sense be called indirectly 'Christological', certainly not in the sense presupposed by Vischer, but in a sense rather more like the subtle understanding of O. Procksch. See above pp. 32f.

Notes to Chapter 4

1. One might, of course, ask in what sense such endeavours are properly called 'biblical *theology*'. It could be argued that 'theology' is not, in fact, a very precise designation for historical studies of the sort mentioned, since the main themes of the biblical literature may not all be exclusively 'theological'. However, the dominant ideas found in the Bible are undoubtedly of a 'religious' nature. And more important still, granted that the contents of the Bible are of decisive significance for Christian teaching and practice (and to explain this is, as I have argued, the task of systematic theology), any serious study of the biblical literature, striving to interpret and understand the texts properly, fully deserves the designation 'theology'.

2. L. Perlitt, *Bundestheologie im Alten Testament* (WMANT, 36; 1969).

3. Von Rad, 'Offene Fragen im Umkreis einer Theologie des Alten Testaments', *ThLZ* 88 (1963), p.405. Cf. *Theology*, II, p.414. See also the very just observations by P. Wernberg-Møller, 'Is There an Old Testament Theology?', *The Hibbert Journal* 59 (1960), pp. 21-29; and cf. S. Wagner, '"Biblische Theologien" und "Biblische Theologie"', *ThLZ* 103 (1978), pp. 787-90.

4. A similar course is adopted by E. Nielsen, *Det gamle Israels religion*

(4th edn; 1979).

5. Naturally, there are also connections between Old Testament theology and the history of Israelite religion, although the subject matter of Old Testament theology is not the religion of Israel as such, but the religious contents of the Old Testament writings. In practice, the Old Testament is the main source and in many instances the only written source upon which our knowledge of Israelite religion can be based.

6. Barr, 'Revelation Through History in the Old Testament and in Modern Theology', *Interpretation* 17 (1963), pp. 193-205 (= *Princeton Seminary Bulletin* 56 [1963], pp. 4-14 = M.E. Marty and D.G. Peerman, *New Theology No. 1* [1964], pp. 60-74); *Old and New in Interpretation* (1966), esp. pp. 65-102.

7. B. Albrektson, *History and the Gods* (Coniectanea Biblica, Old Testament Series, 1; 1967).

8. See especially the collection of H.H. Schmid's essays in his *Altorientalische Welt in der alttestamentlichen Theologie* (1974).

9. Zimmerli, *Grundriss der alttestamentlichen Theologie* (3rd edn; 1982) (ET, *Old Testament Theology in Outline* [1978]).

10. Westermann, *Theologie des Alten Testaments in Grundzügen* (1978) (ET, *Elements of Old Testament Theology* [1982]). See also the remarks by W. Brueggemann, 'A Convergence in Recent Old Testament Theologies', *JSOT* 18 (1980), pp. 2-18.

11. As to the possible confusion caused by this rather flexible terminology, see Schmid, *Altorientalische Welt*, pp. 136-38.

12. See Schmid, 'Altorientalisch-alttestamentliche Weisheit und ihr Verhältnis zur Geschichte', *Altorientalische Welt*, pp. 64-90, esp. pp. 82-87.

13. Zimmerli, 'Zur Struktur der alttestamentlichen Weisheit', *ZAW* 51 (1933), pp. 117-204.

14. Von Rad, *Theologie*, I, pp. 430-53 (ET I, pp. 418-41).

15. The text of Amenemope is available in English translation in *ANET* (3rd edn; 1969), pp. 421-24, and in M. Lichtheim, *Ancient Egyptian Literature*, II (1976), pp. 146-63.

16. Cf. W. McKane, *Proverbs. A New Approach* (1970), esp. pp. 1-10.

17. The relevant Sumerian and Babylonian texts are available in English translation in *ANET* (3rd edn; 1969), pp. 589-91, 596-600, 601-604.

18. See H. Gunkel, 'Die Psalmen', *Reden und Aufsätze* (1913), pp. 92-123; H. Gunkel and J. Begrich, *Einleitung in die Psalmen* (1933); H. Gunkel, *Die Psalmen* (5th edn: 1968).

19. See S. Mowinckel, *Psalmenstudien*, I-VI (1921-1924); *The Psalms in Israel's Worship*, I-II (1962).

20. Cf. the most recent standard commentary on the Psalter, H.-J. Kraus, *Psalmen*, I-II (BKAT, 15/1; 5th edn; 1978).

21. Cf. Lam. 2.7; 4.20.

22. H.W. Wolff, 'Das Kerygma des Jahwisten', *EvTh* 24 (1964), pp. 73-

23. See R. Rendtorff, *Das überlieferungsgeschichtliche Problem des Pentateuch* (BZAW, 147; 1977), esp. pp. 86-112.

24. See the illustrative remarks by J. Wellhausen in his *Prolegomena zur Geschichte Israels* (5th edn; 1899), pp. 3f. (ET, *Prolegomena to the History of Israel* [1885], pp. 2-4).

25. See e.g. E. Würthwein, 'Amos-Studien', *ZAW* 62 (1950), pp. 10-52; H. Graf Reventlow, *Wächter über Israel* (BZAW, 82; 1962); *Das Amt des Propheten bei Amos* (FRLANT, 80; 1962); *Liturgie und prophetisches Ich bei Jeremia* (1963); R.E. Clements, *Prophecy and Covenant* (SBT, 43; 1965), esp. pp. 69-85.

26. See Exod. 22.15-16; and cf. Deut. 22.23-29.

27. A. Alt, 'Die Ursprünge des israelitischen Rechts', *Kleine Schriften zur Geschichte des Volkes Israel*, I (1953), pp. 278-332.

28. The analogy found by some scholars in the stipulations of Hittite suzerainty treaties seems very strained indeed. See the refutation by Gerstenberger, *Wesen und Herkunft*, pp. 96-105.

29. Von Rad, *Theologie*, II, pp. 86f. (ET II, p. 77).

30. For a recent survey of the Mari texts, with ample bibliography, see F. Noort, *Untersuchungen zum Gottesbescheid in Mari* (Alter Orient und Altes Testament, 202; 1977).

BIBLIOGRAPHY

Albrektson, Bertil, *History and the Gods. An Essay on the Idea of Historical Events as Divine Manifestations in the Ancient Near East and in Israel* (Coniectanea Biblica; Old Testament Series, 1; Lund, 1967).

Alt, Albrecht, 'Die Ursprünge des israelitischen Rechts', A. Alt, *Kleine Schriften zur Geschichte des Volkes Israel*, I (München, 1953), pp. 278-332.

Barr, James, *The Semantics of Biblical Language* (Oxford, 1961).

—'Revelation Through History in the Old Testament and in Modern Theology', *Interpretation* 17 (1963), pp. 193-205. (= *Princeton Seminary Bulletin* 56 [1963], pp. 4-14 = Martin E. Marty & Dean G. Peerman, *New Theology 1* [New York, 1964], pp. 60-74).

—*Old and New in Interpretation. A Study of the Two Testaments* (London, 1966).

—'Trends and Prospects in Biblical Theology', *JTS* 25 (1974), pp. 265-82.

—'Biblical Theology', *IDB Supplementary Volume* (Nashville, 1976), pp. 104-11.

—*The Scope and Authority of the Bible* (Explorations in Theology, 7; London, 1980).

—'Childs' Introduction to the Old Testament as Scripture', *JSOT* 16 (1980), pp. 12-23.

—*Holy Scripture. Canon, Authority, Criticism* (Oxford, 1983).

Barton, John, *Reading the Old Testament. Method in Biblical Study* (London, 1984).

Baumgärtel, Friedrich, *Die Bedeutung des Alten Testaments für den Christen* (Schwerin i. Mecklb., 1925).

—*Ist die Kritik am Alten Testament berechtigt? Notwendigkeit, Wesen und Nutzen historisch-kritischer Betrachtung des Alten Testaments* (Schwerin i. Mecklb., 1927).

—*Die Eigenart der alttestamentlichen Frömmigkeit* (Schwerin i. Mecklb., 1932).

—'Erwägungen zur Darstellung der Theologie des Alten Testaments', *ThLZ* 76 (1951), pp. 257-72.

—*Verheissung. Zur Frage des evangelischen Verständnisses des Alten Testaments* (Gütersloh, 1952).

—'Ohne Schlüssel vor der Tür des Wortes Gottes?', *EvTh* 13 (1953), pp. 413-21.

—'Das alttestamentliche Geschehen als "heilsgeschichtliches" Geschehen', *Geschichte und Altes Testament. Albrecht Alt zum siebzigsten Geburtstag* (BHTh, 16; Tübingen, 1953), pp. 13-28.

—'Der Dissensus im Verständnis des Alten Testaments', *EvTh* 14 (1954), pp. 298-313.

—'Das hermeneutische Problem des Alten Testaments', *ThLZ* 79 (1954), pp. 199-211 (= C. Westermann, *Probleme alttestamentlicher Hermeneutik* [1960], pp. 114-39; ET, 'The Hermeneutical Problem of the Old Testament', C. Westermann, *Essays on Old Testament Interpretation* [1963], pp. 134-59).

—'Gerhard von Rads "Theologie des Alten Testaments"', *ThLZ* 86 (1961), pp. 801-16, 895-908.

—'Der Tod des Religionsstifters', *KuD* 9 (1963), pp. 223-33.

—'Das Offenbarungszeugnis des Alten Testaments im Lichte der religionsgeschichtlich-vergleichenden Forschung', *ZThK* 64 (1967), pp. 393-422.

Bornkamm, Heinrich, *Luther und das Alte Testament* (Tübingen, 1948).

Brueggemann, Walter, 'A Convergence in Recent Old Testament Theologies', *JSOT* 18 (1980), pp. 2-18.

Bultmann, Rudolf, 'Die Bedeutung des Alten Testaments für den christlichen Glauben', R. Bultmann, *Glauben und Verstehen*, I (5th edn; Tübingen, 1964 [1st edn, 1933]), pp. 313-36 (ET, 'The Significance of the Old Testament for the Christian Faith', Bernhard W. Anderson, *The Old Testament and Christian Faith. Essays by Rudolf Bultmann and others* [London, 1964], pp. 8-35).

—'Weissagung und Erfüllung', *StTh* 2 (1948), pp. 21-44 (= *ZThK* 47 [1950], pp. 360-83 = R. Bultmann, *Glauben und Verstehen*, II [3rd edn; Tübingen 1961], pp. 162-86 = C. Westermann, *Probleme alttestamentlicher Hermeneutik* [1960], pp. 28-53; ET, 'Prophecy and Fulfillment', R. Bultmann, *Essays Philosophical and Theological* [London, 1955], pp. 182-208 = C. Westermann, *Essays on Old Testament Interpretation* [1963], pp. 50-75).

Childs, Brevard S, *Biblical Theology in Crisis* (Philadelphia, 1970).

—*Introduction to the Old Testament as Scripture* (London, 1979).

—*The New Testament as Canon: An Introduction* (London, 1984).

Clements, Ronald E, *Prophecy and Covenant* (SBT, 43; London, 1965).

—*Old Testament Theology. A Fresh Approach* (London, 1978).

Conzelmann, Hans, 'Fragen an Gerhard von Rad', *EvTh* 24 (1964), pp. 113-25.

Ebeling, Gerhard, 'Die Bedeutung der historisch-kritischen Methode für die protestantische Theologie und Kirche', *ZThK* 47 (1950), pp. 1-46 (= G. Ebeling, *Wort und Glaube* [2nd edn; Tübingen, 1962], pp. 1-49; ET, 'The Significance of the Critical Historical Method for Church and Theology in Protestantism', G. Ebeling, *Word and Faith* [London, 1963], pp. 17-61).

—'The Meaning of "Biblical Theology"', *JTS* 6 (1955), pp. 210-25 (= G. Ebeling, *Word and Faith* [London, 1963], pp. 79-97. German version, 'Was heisst "Biblische Theologie"?', G. Ebeling, *Wort und Glaube* [2nd edn; Tübingen, 1962], pp. 69-89).

Eichrodt, Walther, *Theologie des Alten Testaments*, I-III (Leipzig, 1933-1939) (ET, *Theology of the Old Testament*, I-II [London, 1961-1967]).

—'Ist die typologische Exegese sachgemässe Exegese?' *ThLZ* 81 (1956), pp. 641-54 (= *VTS* 4 [1957] pp. 161-80 = C. Westermann, *Probleme alttestamentlicher Hermeneutik* [1960], pp. 205-26; ET, 'Is Typological Exegesis an Appropriate Method?' C. Westermann, *Essays on Old Testament Interpretation* [1963], pp. 224-45).

Eissfeldt, Otto, 'Israelitisch-jüdische Religionsgeschichte und alttestamentliche Theologie', *ZAW* 44 (1926), pp. 1-12 (= O. Eissfeldt, *Kleine Schriften*, I [Tübingen, 1962], pp. 105-14).

Eldredge, Laurence, see Sandys-Wunsch, John.

Fohrer, Georg, *Theologische Grundstrukturen des Alten Testaments* (Berlin and New York, 1972).

Gabler, Johann Philipp, 'De iusto discrimine theologiae biblicae et dogmaticae regundisque recte utriusque finibus', *Opuscula academica, Kleinere theologische Schriften*, II (Ulm, 1831), pp. 179-98.

Gerstenberger, Erhard, *Wesen und Herkunft des 'apodiktischen Rechts'* (WMANT, 20; Neukirchen, 1965).

Gese, Hartmut, 'Erwägungen zur Einheit der biblischen Theologie', *ZThK* 67 (1970), pp. 417-36 (= *Vom Sinai zum Zion. Alttestamentliche Beiträge zur biblischen Theologie* [BEvTh 64; München, 1974], pp. 11-30).

—*Zur biblischen Theologie. Alttestamentliche Vorträge* (BEvTH 78; München,

1977).

Gunkel, Hermann, 'Die Psalmen', *Reden und Aufsätze* (Göttingen, 1913), pp. 92-123.

—Gunkel, H. and J. Begrich, *Einleitung in die Psalmen* (Göttinger Handkommentar zum Alten Testament, Ergänzungsband zur II. Abteilung; Göttingen, 1933).

—*Die Psalmen* (5th edn; Göttingen, 1968).

Gunneweg, Antonius H.J., '"Theologie des Alten Testaments" oder "Biblische Theologie"?, A.H.J. Gunneweg and O. Kaiser, *Textgemäss. Aufsätze und Beiträge zur Hermeneutik des Alten Testaments* (Göttingen, 1979), pp. 39-46.

Hasel, Gerhard, F., 'The Problem of the Center in the OT Theology Debate', *ZAW* 86 (1974), pp. 65-82.

—*Old Testament Theology: Basic Issues in the Current Debate* (2nd edn; Grand Rapids, 1975).

—'A Decade of OT Theology: Retrospect and Prospect', *ZAW* 93 (1981), pp. 165-83.

Herrmann, Siegfried, 'Die konstruktive Restauration. Das Deuteronomium als Mitte biblischer Theologie', H.W. Wolff, *Probleme biblischer Theologie* (1971), pp. 155-70.

Hesse, Franz, 'Die Erforschung der Geschichte Israels als theologische Aufgabe', *KuD* 4 (1958), pp. 1-19.

—'Kerygma oder geschichtliche Wirklichkeit? Kritische Fragen zu Gerhard von Rads "Theologie des Alten Testaments, I. Teil"', *ZThK* 57 (1960), pp. 17-26.

—'Zur Frage der Wertung und der Geltung alttestamentlicher Texte', C. Westermann, *Probleme alttestamentlicher Hermeneutik* (1960), pp. 266-94 (ET, 'The Evaluation and the Authority of Old Testament Texts', C. Westermann, *Essays on Old Testament Interpretation* [1963], pp. 285-313).

—*Das Alte Testament als Buch der Kirche* (Gütersloh, 1966).

—*Abschied von der Heilsgeschichte* (ThSt, 108; Zürich, 1971).

Honecker, Martin, 'Zum Verständnis der Geschichte in Gerhard von Rads Theologie des Alten Testaments', *EvTh* 23 (1963), pp. 143-68.

Jacob, Edmond, *Théologie de l'Ancien Testament* (Neuchatel, 1955) (ET, *Theology of the Old Testament* [3rd edn; London, 1964]).

—'De la théologie de l'Ancien Testament à la théologie biblique', *RHPhR* 57 (1977), pp. 513-18.

Jensen, Jørgen I, 'Literaturkritische Herausforderungen an die Theologie. Biblische Formprobleme', *EvTh* 41 (1981), pp. 377-401.

Jepsen, Alfred, 'Probleme der Auslegung des Alten Testaments', *ZSth* 23 (1954), pp. 373-86.

Käsemann, Ernst, *Das Neue Testament als Kanon. Dokumentation und kritische Analyse zur gegenwärtigen Diskussion* (Göttingen, 1970).

Keller, Carl A, 'Gerhard von Rad, Theologie des Alten Testament', *ThZ* 14 (1958), pp. 306-309.

Koch, Klaus, 'Der Tod des Religionsstifters', *KuD* 8 (1962), pp. 100-23.

Koch, Klaus, see also Rendtorff, Rolf.

Kraus, Hans-Joachim, 'Gespräch mit Martin Buber', *EvTh* 12 (1952/53), pp. 59-77.

—*Die biblische Theologie. Ihre Geschichte und Problematik* (Neukirchen-Vluyn, 1970).

—'Theologie als Traditionsbildung?' H. Haacker et al., *Biblische Theologie heute* (Biblisch-theologische Studien, 1; Neukirchen-Vluyn, 1977), pp. 61-73.

—*Psalmen*, I-II (BKAT 15/1. 5th edn; Neukirchen-Vluyn, 1978).

Lichtheim, Miriam, *Ancient Egyptian Literature. A Book of Readings. II. The New Kingdom* (Berkeley, Los Angeles and London, 1976).

McKane, William, *Proverbs. A New Approach* (Old Testament Library; London, 1970).

Mildenberger, Friedrich, *Gottes Tat im Wort. Erwägungen zur alttestamentlichen Hermeneutik als Frage nach der Einheit der Geschichte* (Gütersloh, 1964).

Mowinckel, Sigmund, *Psalmenstudien*, I-VI (Kristiania, 1921-1924).

—*The Psalms in Israel's Worship*, I-II (Oxford, 1962).

Nielsen, Eduard, *Det gamle Israels religion* (4th edn; Copenhagen, 1979).

—'The Traditio-historical Study of the Pentateuch since 1945, with special Emphasis on Scandinavia', E. Nielsen, *Law, History, and Tradition. Selected Essays by Eduard Nielsen* (Copenhagen, 1983), pp. 138-54 (= Knud Jeppesen and Benedikt Otzen, *The Productions of Time: Tradition History in Old Testament Scholarship* [Sheffield, 1984], pp. 11-28).

Noort, Edward, *Untersuchungen zum Gottesbescheid in Mari. Die 'Mariprophetie' in der alttestamentlichen Forschung* (Alter Orient und Altes Testament, 202; Neukirchen-Vluyn, 1977).

Noth, Martin, 'Die Vergegenwärtigung des Alten Testaments in der Verkündigung', *EvTh* 12 (1952/53), pp. 6-17 (= C. Westermann, *Probleme alttestamentlicher Hermeneutik* [1960], pp. 54-68; ET, 'The "Re-presentation" of the Old Testament in Proclamation', *Interpretation* 15 [1961], pp. 50-60 = C. Westermann, *Essays on Old Testament Interpretation* [1963], pp. 76-88).

Pannenberg, Wolfhart, *Offenbarung als Geschichte* (KuD, Beiheft 1; Göttingen, 1961 [2nd edn, 1963]) (ET, *Revelation as History* [London and Sidney, 1969]).

—'Kerygma und Geschichte', R. Rendtorff and K. Koch, *Studien zur Theologie der alttestamentlichen Überlieferungen* (1961), pp. 129-40 (ET, 'Kerygma and History', W. Pannenberg, *Basic Questions in Theology*, I [London, 1970], pp. 81-95).

—'Glaube und Wirklichkeit im Denken Gerhard von Rads', H.W. Wolff, R. Rendtorff and W. Pannenberg, *Gerhard von Rad. Seine Bedeutung für die Theologie. Drei Reden* (München, 1973), pp. 37-54.

Perlitt, Lothar, *Bundestheologie im Alten Testament* (WMANT, 36; Neukirchen-Vluyn, 1969).

Procksch, Otto, *Theologie des Alten Testaments* (Gütersloh, 1950).

Rad, Gerhard von, *Das formgeschichtliche Problem des Hexateuch* (BWANT, 78; Stuttgart, 1938) (= G. von Rad, *Gesammelte Studien zum Alten Testament* [Theologische Bücherei, 8; München, 1958], pp. 9-86; ET, 'The Form-Critical Problem of the Hexateuch', G. von Rad, *The Problem of the Hexateuch and other essays* [Edinburgh and London, 1965], pp. 1-78).

—'Typologische Auslegung des Alten Testaments', *EvTh* 12 (1952/53), pp. 17-33 (Abridged version, 'Das Alte Testament ist ein Geschichtsbuch', C. Westermann, *Probleme alttestamentlicher Hermeneutik* [1960], pp. 11-17; ET, 'Typological Interpretation of the Old Testament', *Interpretation* 15 [1961], pp. 174-92 = C. Westermann, *Essays on Old Testament Interpretation* [1963], pp. 17-39).

—'Verheissung. Zum gleichnamigen Buch Friedrich Baumgärtels', *EvTh* 13 (1953), pp. 406-13.

—*Theologie des alten Testaments*. I. *Die Theologie der geschichtlichen Überlieferungen Israels* (München, 1957 [6th edn, 1969]); II. *Die Theologie der prophetischen Überlieferungen Israels* (München, 1961 [5th edn, 1968]) (ET, *Old Testament Theology*. I *The Theology of Israel's Historical Traditions* [Edinburgh and London, 1962]; II. *The Theology of Israel's Prophetic Traditions* [Edinburgh and London, 1965]).

—'Offene Fragen im Umkreis einer Theologie des alten Testaments', *ThLZ* 88 (1963), pp. 401-18.

—'Antwort auf Conzelmanns Fragen', *EvTh* 24 (1964), pp. 388-94.

—*Weisheit in Israel* (Neukirchen-Vluyn, 1970) (ET, *Wisdom in Israel* [London, 1972]).

Rendtorff, Rolf, 'Hermeneutik des Alten Testaments als Frage nach der Geschichte', *ZThK* 57 (1960), pp. 27-40.

—'"Offenbarung" im Alten Testament', *ThLZ* 85 (1960), pp. 833-38.

—'Die Offenbarungsvorstellungen im Alten Israel', W. Pannenberg, *Offenbarung als Geschichte* (KuD, Beiheft 1; 1961), pp. 21-41 (ET, 'The Concept of Revelation in Ancient Israel', W. Pannenberg, *Revelation as History* [1969], pp. 23-53).

—Rendtorff, R. and K. Koch, *Studien zur Theologie der alttestamentlichen Überlieferungen* (Neukirchen, 1961).

—'Geschichte und Überlieferung', R. Rendtorff and K. Koch, *Studien zur Theologie der alttestamentlichen Überlieferungen* (1961), pp. 81-94.

—'Geschichte und Wort im Alten Testament', *EvTh* 22 (1962), pp. 621-49.

—*Das überlieferungsgeschichtliche Problem des Pentateuch* (BZAW, 147; Berlin and New York, 1977).

Reventlow, Henning Graf, 'Grundfragen der alttestamentlichen Theologie im Lichte der neueren deutschen Forschung', *ThZ* 17 (1961), pp. 81-98.

—*Wächter über Israel. Ezechiel und seine Tradition* (BZAW, 82; Berlin, 1962).

—*Das Amt des Propheten bei Amos* (FRLANT, 80; Göttingen, 1962).

—*Liturgie und prophetisches Ich bei Jeremia* (Gütersloh, 1963).

—*Hauptprobleme der alttestamentlichen Theologie im 20. Jahrhundert* (Erträge der Forschung, 173; Darmstadt, 1982) (ET, *Problems of Old Testament Theology in the Twentieth Century* [London, 1985]).

—*Hauptprobleme der Biblischen Theologie im 20. Jahrhundert* (Erträge der Forschung, 203; Darmstadt, 1983).

Rose, Martin, *Deuteronomist und Jahwist. Untersuchungen zu den Berührungspunkten beider Literaturwerke* (AThANT, 67; Zürich, 1981).

Rost, Leonhard, 'Das kleine geschichtliche Credo', L. Rost, *Das kleine Credo und andere Studien zum Alten Testament* (Heidelberg, 1965), pp. 11-25.

Ruler, Arnold A. van, *Die christliche Kirche und das Alte Testament* (BEvTh, 23; München, 1955).

Sandys-Wunsch, John and Laurence Eldredge, 'J.P. Gabler and the Distinction between Biblical and Dogmatic Theology: Translation, Commentary, and Discussion of his Originality', *SJT* 33 (1980), pp. 133-58.

Schmid, Hans Heinrich, *Altorientalische Welt in der alttestamentlichen Theologie. Sechs Aufsätze* (Zürich, 1974).

—*Der sogenannte Jahwist. Beobachtungen und Fragen zur Pentateuchforschung* (Zürich, 1976).

Schmidt, Ludwig, 'Die Einheit zwischen Altem und Neuem Testament im Streit zwischen Friedrich Baumgärtel und Gerhard von Rad', *EvTh* 35 (1975), pp. 119-39.

Smend, Rudolf, 'Johann Philipp Gablers Begründung der biblischen Theologie', *EvTh* 22 (1962), pp. 345-57.

—*Die Mitte des Alten Testaments* (ThSt, 101; Zürich, 1970).

Steuernagel, Carl, 'Alttestamentliche Theologie und alttestamentliche Religionsgeschichte', Karl Budde, *Vom Alten Testament. Karl Marti zum siebzigsten Geburtstage gewidmet* (BZAW, 41; Giessen, 1925), pp. 266-73.

Vischer, Wilhelm, *Das Christuszeugnis des Alten Testaments. I. Das Gesetz* (München, 1934); II. *Die Propheten* (Zürich, 1942).

Vriezen, Th. C, *Theologie des Alten Testaments in Grundzügen* (Wageningen and

Neukirchen, 1956) (ET, *An Outline of Old Testament Theology* [2nd edn; Oxford, 1970]).

Wagner, Siegfried, '"Biblische Theologien" und "Biblische Theologie"', *ThLZ* 103 (1978), pp. 785-98.

Wellhausen, Julius, *Prolegomena zur Geschichte Israels* (5th edn; Berlin, 1899) (ET, *Prolegomena to the History of Israel with a reprint of the article ISRAEL from the 'Encyclopaedia Britannica'* [Edinburgh, 1885]).

Wernberg-Møller, Preben, 'Is There An Old Testament Theology?', *The Hibbert Journal* 59 (1960), pp. 21-29.

Westermann, Claus, *Probleme alttestamentlicher Hermeneutik. Aufsätze zum Verstehen des Alten Testaments* (Theologische Bücherei, 11; München, 1960) (ET, *Essays on Old Testament Interpretation* [London, 1963]).

—*Theologie des Alten Testaments in Grundzügen* (Grundrisse zum Alten Testament, ATD, Ergänzungsreihe, 6; Göttingen, 1978) (ET, *Elements of Old Testament Theology* [Atlanta, 1982]).

Wolff, Hans Walter, 'Der grosse Jesreeltag (Hosea 2,13). Methodische Erwägungen zur Auslegung einer alttestamentlichen Perikope', *EvTh* 12 (1952/53), pp. 78-104.

—'Zur Hermeneutik des Alten Testaments', *EvTh* 16 (1956), pp. 337-70 (= C. Westermann, *Probleme alttestamentlicher Hermeneutik* [1960], pp. 140-80; ET, 'The Hermeneutics of the Old Testament', *Interpretation* 15 [1961], pp. 439-72 = C. Westermann, *Essays on Old Testament Interpretation* [1963], pp. 160-99).

—'Das Kerygma des Jahwisten', *EvTh* 24 (1964), pp. 73-98.

—*Probleme biblischer Theologie. Gerhard von Rad zum 70. Geburtstag* (München, 1971).

Wright, G. Ernest, *God Who Acts. Biblical Theology as Recital* (SBT, 8; London, 1952).

Würthwein, Ernst, 'Amos-Studien', *ZAW* 62 (1950), pp. 10-52.

Zimmerli, Walther, 'Zur Struktur der alttestamentlichen Weisheit', *ZAW* 51 (1933), pp. 177-204.

—'Verheissung und Erfüllung', *EvTh* 12 (1952/53), pp. 34-59 (= C. Westermann, *Probleme alttestamentlicher Hermeneutik* [1960], pp. 69-101; ET, 'Promise and Fulfillment', *Interpretation* 15 [1961], pp. 310-38 = C. Westermann, *Essays on Old Testament Interpretation* [1963], pp. 89-122).

—'"Offenbarung" im Alten Testament. Ein Gespräch mit R. Rendtorff', *EvTh* 22 (1962), pp. 15-31.

—'G. von Rad, Theologie des Alten Testaments', *VT* 13 (1963), pp. 100-11.

—'Erwägungen zur Gestalt einer alttestamentlichen Theologie', *ThLZ* 98 (1973), pp. 81-98.

—'Zum Problem der "Mitte des Alten Testaments"', *EvTh* 35 (1975), pp. 97-118.

—*Grundriss der alttestamentlichen Theologie* (Theologische Wissenschaft, 3; 3rd edn; Stuttgart, 1982 [1st edn, 1972]) (ET, *Old Testament Theology in Outline* [Edinburgh, 1978]).

INDEX OF AUTHORS